The International Cultivators Handbook

By Bill Drake
Copyright © Bill Drake 1974-2010
Second Edition
Revised & Expanded
All Rights Reserved
Some Illustrations by Pat Krug
From "Medicinal Marijuana Foods" by Bill Drake

- Introduction to the Second Edition 1
  - The Criminalization of Natural Medicines 3
- SECTION ONE: TRADITIONAL PREPARATIONS & USES OF CANNABIS 6
  - The Manufacture of Flat and Round Ganja in India 6
  - Preparation of Hashish in Lebanon 9
  - Balouchistan (Southern Pakistan) Hash Processing 10
  - Himalayan Cannabis Processing – Urgum & Yarkand 11
  - Northern Bengal Cannabis Cultivation Techniques 14
  - Javadi Hills Cannabis Processing Techniques 16
  - The Pit-Planted Ganja of Mysore 17
  - Traumatizing Cannabis For Higher Yield – Folk Techniques 18
    - The Traumatic Basket 20
  - A Simple, Objective Test for Cannabis Potency 20
  - Grades of Egyptian Hashish 21
    - Strep Throat? Use Dope. 22
  - Cannabis In Folk Medicine Traditions 27
  - Cannabis As A Potent Old Age Treatment 32
- SECTION TWO: THE CULTIVATION AND USE OF COCA 35
  - Introduction 35
  - In Search of the Elusive Coca Plant 36
  - Scientific & Personal Observations on Medicinal Coca 38
    - A Physician's Summary Of the Medical Benefits 49
  - Erythroxylon 52
    - Some Regional Variations of Coca 53
  - Commentaries on the Cultivation Of Coca 55
  - The Gathering & Drying Of Coca 57
  - Traditional Indian Coca Cultivation 58
    - Environmental Conditions 58
    - Types of Earth Most Suitable 58
    - The Importance of Humidity 59
    - Protecting Seeds & Seedlings 60
    - Planting Out & Cultivating Coca 60
    - The Processes of Harvesting 61
  - Selecting Coca Seeds For Planting 63
  - Pests & Predators of the Coca Plant 64
  - Summary Of Coca Cultivation Techniques 65
  - The World of Vin Mariani 68
    - Of Coca And Its True Therapeutic Properties. 68
    - Proper Cultivation Techniques 69
    - Harvesting For Maximum Purity & Potency 69
    - Preparation of the Harvest 71
- SECTION THREE: CULTIVATION & USE OF THE OPIUM POPPY 72
  - A Poem On The Cultivation Of The Medicinal Poppy 73
  - The Opium Poppy – A Brief Overview 74
    - Identification of the Opium Poppy 74
    - Cultivation of the Opium Poppy 76
  - Country-Specific Cultivation Techniques 77
    - Bulgarian Cultivation Techniques 77
    - Balkan Cultivation of the Opium Poppy 79
    - Turkish Opium Poppy Cultivation Techniques 80
  - Steps In Cultivation 81
    - A. General observations 81
    - B. Time of sowing 81
    - C. Method of sowing 82
    - D. Various stages of growth 83
    - E. Work to be done during growth period 83

F. The enemies of the poppy 84
Indian Opium Cultivation & Preparation Techniques 85
    The Critical Phase and Its Signs 86
Current Indian Opium Varieties 87
Incising and Harvesting Techniques In Four Countries 89
    Turkey 89
    Preparing Raw Opium 92
    Bulgaria 93
    Former Yugoslavia (The Balkans) 93
    India 94
Your Seed Harvest 94
    A Quick Note on Degeneration 95
APPENDIX ONE: SECRETS OF AN OPIUM-GROWING MASTER 96
    Introduction & Summary of Findings 99
    Section 1: The Soils of the Deegah Gardens: their State of Cultivation etc. 103
    Section 2: The Soil 104
    Section 3: The Waters used in Irrigation 105
    Section 4: Weather Characteristics for the Poppy Season 1876-77 106
    Section 5: The Sowing Season, and the Allotment of Land etc. 109
    Section 6: The Germination of the Seed 111
    Section 7: The Season of the Plants Growth, and General Condition of the Crop 112
    Section 8: The Drug Collecting Season and Produce of the Several Varieties 115
    Section 9: Pussewa: it's Nature and Origin 134
    Section 10: The Seed Harvest: the Selection of the Capsules and the Storage of the Seed 138
    Section 11: The Diseases and Injuries of the Crop, by Parasitic Fungi, Insects, etc. 140
APPENDIX TWO: TRADITIONAL USES OF CANNABIS, OPIUM AND COCA 145
    Andean Indians and their Poporo 145
    Coca Leaf Tea & America's Morbid Obesity 146
    Opium Delights 147
    Cannabis Preparations 148
APPENDIX THREE: A COMMENTARY ON THE BEING ELECTRIC 151
Index To Contents 171

PLEASE NOTE: Nothing in this book is intended as a recommendation that anyone violate any US laws against the production or possession of illegal drugs. All techniques and methods described are a matter of historical record and are traditional in much of the world. This book is intended primarily to inform and enlighten the reader who is interested in how other people in other times have grown and used Opium, Coca and Hashish as natural medicines.

It is also intended as a statement of the author's personal advocacy for changing the US laws that prohibit Americans from exercising their legitimate right to grow and consume their own medicinal plants of whatever kind they choose as free and independent citizens.

Introduction to the Second Edition

I wrote the first "International Cultivators Handbook" in the early 1970s after six years of traveling around the world in search of traditional techniques for the production of Cannabis, especially in the form of hashish. In those days I was focused strongly on Cannabis, having just written the "Cultivators Handbook of Marijuana" and the "Connoisseur's Handbook of Marijuana". However the more I traveled in South America, the Middle East, India and SE Asia the more intrigued I became with both Coca and Opium. In many of the places I was traveling taking pictures wasn't greeted with smiles and poses – more precisely the sight of my camera got me into a number of pretty touchy situations – and in the course of several years I learned to carry only the cheapest camera, after having several of them smashed or confiscated. However I did manage to get a few good shots in most places and these rather grainy photographs, along with some archival graphics, brought the "International Cultivators Handbook" to life. My good friends at Wingbow Press, the publishing arm of Bookpeople, did a wonderful job of designing a handsome and graphically compelling book and over the years I've heard from quite a few very satisfied readers. "International Cultivators" went out of print in the late 1970s, and I went on to write other books believing that there was little more to say on the subject of traditional methods of cultivating and using these great medicinal plants.

But that was then and this is now. Generations have been born and grown up since the 1960s, and for many of these younger people the criminalized, commercialized versions of cannabis, coca and opium are all they've ever known. Over the years since the late 1960s I've watched, along with millions of other people, how the uber-fascist combination of bloated government agencies, giant corporate squids, and cruel narco-syndicates have taken these great gifts of the natural world – Cannabis, Coca and Opium – and turned them from blessings into curses. Their medicinal properties have been largely ignored, although of course opium compounds play a major role in medicine, and their status as illegal drugs has insured that people who want any of these plants for either health or recreation are effectively prevented from growing their own – although nothing could be easier. Many of us have watched with great satisfaction as the truth about the medical properties of Cannabis has at first slowly and now inexorably made its way into the popular mind. Cannabis is finally on its way to re-acceptance as both a wonderful medicine and a first-class consciousness altering drug.

BRANCH OF COCA PLANT.
Showing Leaf, Flower and Seed.

Coca on the other hand, despite a long and detailed history of medicinal uses in the 18th-19th centuries, has not yet re-entered the popular consciousness as a medicinal plant; rather it has become a recreational powder, controlled by criminal syndicates and protected by corrupted government officials and bankers worldwide. Perhaps it's because the Coca plant, unlike the Cannabis plant, has some very particular requirements regarding soil, climate, and environment that homegrown Coca hasn't spread throughout society the way homegrown Cannabis has. However, given the incredible advances in indoor growing technologies I see no reason at all why Coca plants can't be grown successfully just about anywhere and if fact I'm sure that's exactly what is going on with the criminal syndicates, so there's no reason that individuals who want their own supply of pure, natural coca leaves can't do the same. We'll describe the environmental conditions traditionally required for successful Coca growing, and as you'll see, these conditions can easily be re-created using contemporary indoor growing technology.

On the other hand, nothing could be easier to grow than the Opium Poppy, and there are so many varieties of poppies adapted to cultivation almost anywhere on earth, the only explanation why homegrown opium hasn't yet become a popular phenomenon is because the penalties for growing this most valuable medicinal plant, even for your own private use, are in many places more harsh than for murdering your mother or raping a baby. Nevertheless, opium poppies are quite possibly the most widely grown of the three great medicinal plants in the US, exceeding even Cannabis, simply because they are grown by so many people as ornamentals – people who may or may not know what to do with those plump green capsules that emerge from the base of the flower. Because of all the hypocrisy and deliberately evil machinations of governments, corporations, banks, criminal mobs, and corrupt police worldwide aimed at criminalizing and prohibiting people from having access to these great medicines, I have decided to try to do what I can to once again bring the knowledge of traditional methods of growing and using these great medicinal plants to people of the new generations. **But please make no mistake – in most places you will be taking a substantial risk of going to prison by growing either Coca trees or Poppy plants. Therefore I recommend that you treat the information**

in this book as historical rather than actionable. We can all be thankful that, at least in some places, growing your own Cannabis is no longer an issue.

In the following pages you'll find the original information in the first International Cultivators Handbook, interspersed with new and detailed information on traditional growing techniques from historical sources that were not in the first edition. While the techniques and technology of producing fine quality hashish and Marijuana have evolved at warp speed over the years since this book was first written, back in the days when Afghani hash was king and the first potent little Afghani Indica plants were first being imported into the West coast of the US by adventurous hippie entrepreneurs, the traditional methods of growing and producing Coca and Opium covered in this book deserve to be conserved and remembered, which is why I have updated and expanded the book for re-publication. In the 60s very few Americans other than hippies and GIs knew anything at all about opium, and powder cocaine was the only form of Coca anyone in the US was familiar with, while in much of the rest of the world millions of people had been happily smoking raw opium and chewing Coca leaves for generations. This is the world I traversed at the time, searching for exotic knowledge that, in the time before the Internet, was almost universally unavailable in the developed world. The International Cultivators Handbook is the result of what I found on those long-ago adventures. This updated edition is a collection and analysis of what many, many people have learned over several hundred years regarding the care and cultivation of these great medicinal plants. If you are interested, www.archive.org is an internet address where you can do your own research by downloading literally dozens of old treatises on virtually any historical aspect of Cannabis, Opium, Coca and (for good measure) heirloom tobacco – all for free!

The Criminalization of Natural Medicines

As we move toward legalization of marijuana in the United States, growing the plant becomes more fun and less dangerous, and makes more, not less sense.

When early mapmakers reached the limits of the then-known, yet sought to encompass the whole earth, territories which lay beyond the European pale were posted on the maps with a brief, sufficient warning:

Here Be Dragons

Today man rules all the earth. But the dragon, a shifty beast, seems not in the least disturbed by man's dominion over the old lands. However secure man's hold upon the earth, there always seems to be room for dragons on his maps.

It is incredible that with so many dragons lurking about, men rarely seem to learn from the experiences of other men in dealing with the beasts. Arrogance plays a part in this general failure to exchange knowledge, as does plain ignorance. Moreover, the nature of dragons dictates that they are very personal-antagonists, often requiring that men seek unusual, uncommon means of banishing their menace. In short, the defeat of dragons is a very complex business.

But man is a flexible creature, and over the course of his intellectual evolution he has hit upon several, more-or-less successful approaches to the dragon problem. Western man has established a cult activity which is named science, and through steady application of the special tools of this science he has slain many dragons. The primary tool categories of science are systematic inquiry, precise description, exhaustive analysis of process, and confirmation of results.

However, western man does not have total confidence in his scientific tools; he remains a being subject to impulse, hysteria and superstition when he is confronted with certain forms of the unknown. Nowhere is this primitive reversion more marked than in those areas of life concerned with the consolidation of consciousness.

Here Be Dragons

And here be drugs. Let a new drug slide purposefully into any society, of any period, and most of the people will fall back in disarray, certain that they are about to become a meal. Some others will rush forward, not caring whether it is beast or benefactor, eager only for the sensation of contact. Some will compose songs and poetry, either to celebrate or to propitiate the new artifice. Some will attack, using the old weapons held over from other times, other enemies. Some will see profit, some will see power, and some will see a god.

And some will seek to understand. Of these some will be arrogant, certain that they are unique among people, and they will seek to understand without reference to what other people, of other periods, may have known or discovered. Some will be ignorant, and will assume that there are, in fact, new things under the sun, and that what is new to them is indeed new, and thus will proceed oblivious, to any but their personal path toward understanding. And some will go to the teachers, and to the books to inquire whether others have confronted this dragon before, and what might have been their experience, and how might this learning be applied in this particular place and time. Only then do such people, not necessarily more cautious than their fellows, turn to the work at hand.

Carl Jung wrote that "It would be ridiculous and unwarranted presumption on our part if we imagined that we were more energetic or more intelligent than the men of the past - our material knowledge has increased, not our intelligence." In that vein, it is equally ridiculous and unwarranted to ignore or reject substantive material knowledge assembled by intelligent people of the past when it bears directly upon contemporary problems for which we have developed no adequate solutions. Yet this is most certainly what we have done with marijuana, coca and opium in America.

We have, instead, established and enforced layer upon layer of criminal penalties for the possession, use and transfer of these natural medicines/recreational drugs; we have erected a vast mythology on all sides of the question; we have struggled to rationalize both prohibition and legalization; we have expended wealth, energy and lives in the pursuit and contravention of the laws; we even use military satellites to bust backyard growers; all this without so much as a pause to inquire into the experiences of other people in other places and times. Small wonder this dragon has us backed into a corner. The tide of affairs is changing. The mapmakers are being forced to revise their maps as they discover that not only is this territory not the land of dragons, but that it has a long and continuous history of human habitation. Happily, the civilizations which dwelt in this land have often left records of their experiences, and these documents should prove invaluable in the revision of our mapmakers' maps. Let's begin with an examination of some ancient traditions in what many believe are the heartland and homeland of both Cannabis Sativa and the Opium Poppy – Mother India and the Middle East.

SECTION ONE: TRADITIONAL PREPARATIONS & USES OF CANNABIS

The Manufacture of Flat and Round Ganja in India

It is essential that harvest-time fall in a period of bright sunny weather, since the plants, not all coming to maturity simultaneously, must be manipulated within three or four days of maturity or they lose considerable potency, odor and color. The plants are cut and carried from the fields in bundles, in quantities according to the manufacturer's available facilities and labor force.

The manufacture of flat ganja takes three days and is carried out on a piece of ground near the field with has been specially leveled for the purpose. This working place is called the Chator, or Khola. The number of plants handled in any given three days operation is usually about fifty or sixty substantial females, standing at maturity from ten to twelve feet high.

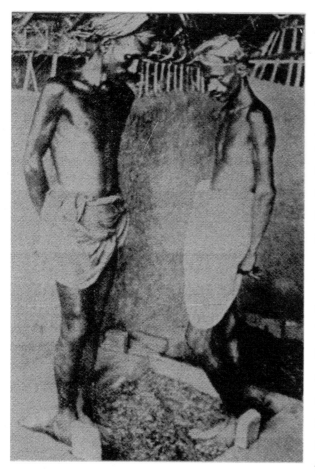

On the first morning the plants are cut, brought to the Chator, and spread individually in the sun, where they lie until early afternoon. They are then cut up into lengths of either one or two feet, depending on the intended size of the finished product. Those pieces having flower spikes are retained; the rest is thrown away, since the twigs and branches without ganja are considered useless, and as much of the woody stems as can be separated without disturbing the flower clusters is also eliminated.

The sorted pieces are then left under the open sky, exposed to the dews of night, until the next day. The following morning the pieces are gathered and tied into small bundles of approximately ten spikes apiece, which are stacked in layers, heads inward and overlapping, in a circular pattern on a piece of raffia matting. As the spikes are being laid on the mat, the men who tread move into action, each man taking approximately sixty degrees of the circle.

Each man takes the spikes one at a time, fixes the outer end with the pressure of one foot and with the other foot begins a rolling, kneading action working progressively toward the inner end of the spike. As new layers of plants are added the balancing required to follow this course of action becomes somewhat precarious, consequently the men who tread are accustomed to form a circle and work in unison, grasping the shoulders of the man on either side and moving in and out together.

When the stack is about a foot and a half high, consisting of four or five layers, the building up process ceases and the men step down. Covering the pile with a couple of mats the treaders take a break by sitting on the mats; this keeps the pile flattened out.

After thirty minutes, the break over, the men remove the mats and each begins taking up pairs of bundles, beating them together vigorously over the sitting mats which have been laid beside the pile.

The beating causes seeds and broken leaves to fall out of the semi-agglutinated spikes, and this chaff is winnowed by specialized workmen for choice seed for next year's crop. The bundles are then replaced on the treading mat and the piling up and massage begins anew. When the pile is again built the men take a second sit-press break and, a half hour later, remove the bundles one by one from the pile. This time the bundles are laid out individually on mats and dressed by the foot technique as is used in treading the collective pile. For each spike bundle the dressing is repeated three times on a side, after which a second beating together of pairs of bundles takes place. By this time it is late afternoon of the second day, and the bundles are then laid out on the grass, covered with mats to prevent the dew from settling upon them, and left for the night.

Next morning the bundles are restacked, treaded, and pressed once, then left in the pile for two hours to absorb the heat of the sun. At 10 a.m. the pile is broken down and the bundles are placed in double facing rows on mats, heads inward the overlapping, and two or three of the heaviest men proceed to trample down the rows with a good deal of force. After trampling both sides of the bundles, they are taken up and very gently beaten to remove the last of the chaff and seeds. The flowering tops are now very hard and firm, and have a distinct flattened shape. The manufacture of flat ganja is thus complete.

For the manufacture of round ganja a rice field is selected as the Chator, and for some reason this Chator is always further from the village than is the case with flat ganja. Huts are usually erected for the workmen so that they stay with the ganja throughout its manufacture. The plants are reaped in the afternoon of the first day and are laid out in the open in the Chator yard overnight, after which the initial sorting takes place in the same fashion as with flat ganja. The lengths into which the plant is cut are much shorter, however, usually not exceeding six inches, and a great deal more effort is expended in separating woody material.

The selected pieces are laid out in the heat of the sun until noon, when the manufacturing process begins.

A long horizontal bamboo pole is tied about four feet about the flat floor of the Chator, affixed firmly to a series of stout upright posts. Mats are spread beneath this bar and the treaders line up on either side, grasping the bar with both hands in a way that allows them to bring maximum weight to bear on the bundles underfoot. For round ganja the bundles are tied at one end only, and are quite loose. The most expert treaders can manage untied bundles, and there is a good deal of side talk and status commentary which goes on among the treaders with regard to their various levels of skill. The first rolling (ekmalai) takes about ten minutes, by which time the bundles are beginning to agglutinate in the distinctive round shape of this type of ganja. The bundles are then left in the sun for twenty minutes and the second rolling (domalai) takes place, this time for about five minutes. After the second foot roll the men sit down and proceed to roll the bundles with their hands, shaping and applying as much pressure as possible. The heads are then left for a half hour in the sun; then taken up again, rolled and pressed with both foot and hand, and left in the sun until late afternoon at which time they are collected, tied loosely in large bundles, and laid out on mats, covered over, for the night.

The third day, in the morning, the bundles are collected and untied, and the spikes left in the sun to dry until midday, at which time they are each inspected for dryness. If they are dry enough they are simply subjected to hand rolling; those with excess moisture are once again laid out beneath the bar and foot massaged, then hand rolled. The third day's work is finished by two o'clock, at which time the bundles are each inspected for any remaining woody projections. This picking is casual, and consumes the bulk of the afternoon, during which time there is usually some sampling by the workers. In late afternoon, the bundles are built in double layered rows, mats placed over them with great stones on top, and they are left for the night.

On the final day of manufacture the bundles are uncovered as soon as the dew has risen and are left in the sun until the heat of the afternoon. They are then inspected for any remaining chaff, given a final hand-rounding, and the manufacture of round ganja is completed.

Preparation of Hashish in Lebanon

Preparation of hashish from the mature, female marijuana plant is a traditional operation in the mountain valleys of Lebanon, the techniques of which have not changed much over the course of thousands of years. The marijuana fields are planted early in the year, and arrive at maturity towards the end of September. The late summer sunlight brings out a subtle color shift, from ocean green to dull amber, in the ripening fields. In the warm winds of late afternoon the resin-heavy marijuana plants nod sluggishly under their load of fruit and leaves.

Harvesters enter the fields stripped to the waist and begin the process of severing the ripe stalks at their base. Rough wooden carts are drawn into the fields on the heels of the harvesters, and the plants are piled into these carts alternating top to bottom. As each cart is filled, it is hitched to a donkey and driven off to the nearby village.

In the center of each village there are specially prepared drying beds of hard-packed clay, surrounded by low walls for protection from the wind and whitewashed so that the heat from the sun is trapped and reflected onto the piles of plants in the center of the floor. The cut marijuana lies on these drying beds for about two weeks, alternately baking in the sun by day, and soaking in the light dew of the nights. Each plant is turned daily, and care is taken that no plant remains on the bottom of a pile for more than a day, for this could lead to onset of a molding process which would spoil the flavor, and ultimately the potency of the leaves.

At the end of the two week drying period, the leaves and their amber cargo are powder-dry. The plants are then carefully carried to specially constructed, sealed beating rooms which have smooth walls, floors and ceilings, and only the one door. Plants are piled in the center of the floor, and the beaters enter the room, which is then sealed from the outside. The beaters are clothed only in loincloths, and wear masks over their mouths and nose to prevent inhalation of the resin powder. Slatted wood flails are used in the beating process.

The first beating raises a dense cloud of resin powder, which settles on the walls, floors, and ceiling and on the bodies of the beaters. If the hashish to be manufactured is intended as premium drug, the beating is stopped at this point and the room is carefully scraped to remove the fine dust, and the bodies of the beaters are scraped clean with the dulled blades of short knives. The debris in the middle of the floor is also processed for fine powder by scrubbing the stems, twigs and leaf fragments over a very fine mesh.

The first-class powder is then set aside, and successively coarser meshes are used in scrubbing the remaining debris until no further powder is obtainable. A less quality-oriented manufacturer will simply lump all of the powder obtained from each successive screening together in one batch, and will often take little care that no twigs, branches or seeds are included in the final product.

The final operation in the manufacture of hashish is to add whatever adulterants are considered useful or traditional. These adulterants serve many purposes. Some serve as flavoring, some disguise the odor of the hashish, some add bulk or color, and some serve as supplementary intoxicants. The adulterated powder is then poured into small, strong linen or canvas bags. These bags often are the traditionally-shaped pantoufle, a foot-shaped mold which results in the final shape of the processed hashish resembling a footpad. One of the traditional smuggling methods for hashish involved hiring people to slip these pantoufles into their shoes and walk across border stations and through customs on a cushion of hashish. While this method is very well known to Middle Eastern customs and police, and while it has fallen into general disuse, it remains a cheap and relatively efficient technique which is still used to some extent, and the pantoufle shape still dominates the manufacturing of hashish in many Lebanese villages.

Once the raw powder has been poured into the bags, they are sewn tightly shut and are placed in a steam cabinet and heated until the powder in the bags has been reduced to a pasty consistency, after which the bags are removed and placed in a press which stamps the manufacturer's seal in the still-warm hashish. The bags are then laid out to cool after which they are ready for shipment.

Balouchistan (Southern Pakistan) Hash Processing

This method, first described by M.D. Hooper in 1908 resembles in many ways the operations employed by Lebanese hashish processors. One takes entire plants, gathered at the point of heavy ripening, and lays them out in the sun to dry until they are crisp to the touch.

The beating chamber is a small room with clean, whitewashed walls, ceiling and floor, all of which are covered with a fine linen. The dried plants are brought into the chamber and laid on the floor in bundles or, alternatively, are laid out upon a smooth wooden bench or table. The beaters are masked to prevent inhalation of the powder arising from the processing; a precaution, no doubt, against one's employees laying down and out on the job. The beating is done with bundles of supple green sticks, very much like the flails used in beating out grain throughout Europe and the east. With vigorous beating, a fine powder rises and fills the room, clinging to the linen sheets. After the point is reached where very little more fine powder can be obtained by further beating, the workers leave the room as quickly as possible, closing the door behind them, and the powder is allowed to settle.

The linen is then stripped from the walls and ceiling, while that on the floor is left and the clinging powder is scraped into leather or skin sacks, and set aside. The linen is replaced, and another round of beating takes place. The powder which arises from this second beating is a bit sparser than the first quality product, and by the time the flailing is over there is a great quantity of debris on the linen on the floor. This time the entire room is stripped, including the floor linen, and the resulting collection is set aside for a screening operation. This consists of passing the debris through a series of progressively finer sieves until the manufacturer obtains whatever grade of powder he feels he can market under his second-grade label.

In some places the operation is repeated a third time to obtain a decidedly inferior grade of powder; in other factories the stuff left after the second beating is given to the employees as their bonus.

First grade powder is usually further processed to form the familiar hashish cake. The powder is poured into linen bags of sufficient strength and thickness to be impermeable. These bags are placed on a rack above a steam bath and are steamed until the contents turn soft. The bags are then taken to a press which forms them into cakes of characteristic shape, and which imprints the manufacturer's seal into the cake. They are then laid back in a cool place to harden, after which they are ready for sale. Depending on the quality of the resin in the plants, this same operation can be repeated with the second grade of powder, though usually such cakes bear an altogether different seal when finished.

Himalayan Cannabis Processing – Urgum & Yarkand

The people of Urgum, a tiny spot at 8000 feet in the central Himalayas, practice a simple form of Charas manufacture. The Cannabis fields of the village surround the temple of Siva and is gathered not only for use by the villagers but also as an offering to be tendered to pilgrims on the trails to Kedarnath and Badrinath which pass through the valley. The female plants (called Sujango) are harvested in November of each year. The flowering tops are broken off in twelve inch lengths, an operation which usually takes place in the morning, the period of greatest dormancy for the plant. These spikes are spread in the sun for twenty four hours, into the heat of the following high noon. The people then gather up loose bundles of the spikes and go down to the temple to begin the work of preparation. Each person takes up one spike at a time and kneads it slowly in his hands with a washing motion. The combination of body heat and massage, and the rays of the clear Himalayan sun cause the spike to become soft, liberating its cargo of amber resin which oozes between the fingers and coats the palms. At intervals a man passes among the people with a knife and scrapes the hands of each person. The remaining flower head is thrown onto a fire in the center of the circle. The simple charas thus made has come to be prized well beyond the little valley called Urgum.

In Yarkand, Ganja is harvested in its seventh month. It is an especially favored crop because it can grow in wasteland as well as interspersed among the village fields and pampered garden crops. After the harvesting, which consists of cutting the whole female plant at the base, the plants are laid upon the roofs of the houses for a month. The plants are turned daily to promote even drying and to give good exposure to the rays of the sun and to the cool, clear air of night. There is apparently no worry about mold as is almost always the case at lower altitudes. When the month is up the plants are taken in to a community beating house with a stone floor where the smaller leaves and seeds are winnowed by light threshing from the more compact flower heads, the woody stalks and stems having first been carefully removed. The flower heads are then placed in a pile and are, one at a time, ground to a powder in a mortar. The powder is then subjected to three screenings using successively finer mesh grades, and the final product is poured into small leather bags and sold to travelling merchants who make the rounds of Yarkand villages at the end of every season. These merchants also buy raw stock and store it in large leather bags through the winter; come June of the year following, they engage workers to do their own sort of processing. The powder obtained from the villagers is poured from the bags onto finely woven mats and left for a full day in the heat of the sun. In the middle of the afternoon the hot powder is taken up, mixed with honey and butter, and hand kneaded into various shapes depending on the eventual market destination. Upon occasion an additional dose of raw powder is added to the kneaded resin/honey mixture to increase potency; in such cases a special seal is affixed to the packets, usually consisting of a bird of Paradise arising from a setting sun.

This high grade Yarkand Charas is rarely seen outside the Himalayas these days; in former times it was a common article of trade as far south as Mysore state in India. When the merchants buy the raw stock from villagers they also store it through the winter and, come June, the spikes are turned out onto mats where they are separated and left to heat in the direct sun for a full day, after which they are hand-picked clean of stalks, trodden underfoot until the resin rises to the surface, then put into specially sewn leather bags which are, when full, rectangular in shape. The warm, clean tops are crammed into the bags, which are then compressed powerfully, with successive layers of spikes being added until the bags become a solid block of crude resin and flower weighing twenty or forty pounds, again depending upon the consignee and eventual market. These Yarkand blocks can be seen in almost all Himalayan and foothill markets, and are fairly common even further afield.

The Bhutia of the high kingdom go more directly to the plant for their Charas. In these mountain valleys the fall of the year is a time of heavy dews, which coincides with the ripe season of the Cannabis plant. At sundown, when a chill creeps into the air and the moisture of the early evening has begun settling on the still warm plants and their coat of resin, the cultivator and his family will go into the fields with baskets of hearth ash and scatter the ash to windward of the clumped plants. Through the night the fine ash will combine with the resin and the dew and, when morning comes, but well before the sun has risen, the people put on rough textured leather jackets and pass through the fields embracing and rubbing against the plants. The jackets are soon laden with the dilute but stabilized resin/ash/dew, which is scraped from each person as he arrives at the field's end. Within several hours, in this manner, a family can collect several pounds of high quality resin without the complicated processing one encounters elsewhere.

Northern Bengal Cannabis Cultivation Techniques

The Bengal Cannabis cultivator generally practices transplantation rather than direct open field sowing of seed. The fields into which the nursery plants are to be placed are taken in hand about the beginning of March, and are ploughed some half-dozen times to remove all traces of the previous crop as well as any weeds which may have intruded during the fallow period. The field is allowed to lie untouched for about a month after the initial working, and then the dressing operations begin. The land chosen is usually a light, dry sandy loam, and is surface dressed with earth taken from ditches at the edge of the field or from nearby low-lying fields. For this top-dressing operation only soil from the top two or three inches of the donor land is used. Also, weeds and turf from the banks and ditches surrounding the recipient field are taken up and thrown into the center of the dressed area. The prepared earth is then allowed to lie for about a week, after which a generous manuring with cow-dung takes place. Another week is allowed to pass, after which the top-dressing and manure is ploughed under. The plowing operation is continued once or twice weekly until the monsoon bursts upon the land. After the rains have begun, the field is alternately ploughed and harrowed once a month until mid-September when, at an appropriate break in the rains, the field receives a second thorough and thick manuring; this manure is ploughed and harrowed under about six times, alternately, over the course of the next few days and, since by this time the rains have stopped, the time for transplantation now comes. The soil of the field is ridged and made ready to receive the seedlings, which are by this time about a month and a half old and from six to ten inches in height. In order to obtain all of the benefits of the breaking up of the soil without at the same time incurring the liabilities of an over-dry bed, the transplanting is carried out on the same day as the final plowing, harrowing and ridging.

A month or so after transplantation, about the middle of October, the fields are carefully weeded and two weeks later, around the first of November, another critical operation is undertaken. The ridges are hoed down as far as permissible without exposing or injuring the roots of the young plants. The reduced ridges are then well-dressed with oilcake and cow-dung, and the ridges rebuilt over the layer of fertilizer.

In the middle of November the plants are trimmed by way of removing their lower branches. This pruning acts to give the plant a pyramidal shape which ensures that the flowering tops will grow closely together. It also makes possible another course of plowing with small ploughs and harrowing with a small ladder between the rows, which operation immediately follows the trimming and is itself followed by another breaking down of the ridges, manuring with cow dung and oil cake, and rebuilding of the ridges.

At this time the Ganja doctor makes his first visit to the fields looking for male plants and abnormal growth of various sorts. He passes through the field breaking over any suspect plants, followed closely by the cultivator who uproots the broken plants and replaces them with fresh nursery stock.

Following the Ganja doctor's first visit the field is irrigated for the first time. Enough water is put on the field to wet the ridges thoroughly without leaving standing water in the furrows. The field is irrigated every two to three weeks from this point until January, and the Ganja doctor makes his rounds every five weeks during the same period. In some areas another round of breaking down, manuring and building up of the ridges takes place between the first and second irrigations.

In the beginning of January the hemp crop begins to flower, and from this time until harvest the cultivator is on the lookout for any abnormal flowers appearing on his female plants, abnormalities which even the Ganja doctor could not possibly have foretold prior to flowering. (For a description of typical Cannabis abnormalities, see The Cultivator's Handbook of Marijuana, an earlier book of mine.)

It should be evident that the Bengalese cultivator treats his hemp crop more in the manner of a garden than a field endeavor. High cultivation in the practices of tilth, manuring and irrigation, united with a careful attention to the prevention of fertilization, forces the plant into production of the narcotic principle to an abnormal degree.

Javadi Hills Cannabis Processing Techniques

The Javadi Hills are a low range in south-central India, covered with a thick jungle growth, among which the Malayli villages are scattered, few of them consisting of more than three or four huts and encompassing one extended family. Each village has a small patch of communal land cleared for cultivation of food crops and, in most cases, for Cannabis cultivation. The Malaylais claim themselves to be related to the Vellala people of the plains but have very little commerce or contact outside of their mountain retreat. They also feel quite superior to the plainspeople, due largely to their superior knowledge of the ways of cultivation of a high grade Ganja plant.

Malaylai cultivation techniques do not vary much from the standard techniques practiced elsewhere in India; however, their processing is a bit different and merits consideration. In harvesting the plants are cut whole, tied into small bundles and carried to the threshing floor of the village. There the flowering tops are stripped from the main stem, and the branches carefully plucked out and discarded. The clean spikes thus obtained are then spread in the sun for the heat of the day and after four or five hours have passed the workers sit down and hand-work each spike, popping out seeds with a quick motion of the thumb and carefully winnowing the smallest of stems. The manufacture then begins.

A closely woven bamboo basket is dusted with powdered leaf collected from the floor. Into the basket a layer of spikes is placed, and these are then trodden under heel by a man who climbs into the basket and supports himself by a staff. If the basket is large enough, two men will climb in and work around, supporting each other by the shoulders. Layer over layer of spikes are successively added and trodden, with a little leaf dust added between layers. When the basket is compacted full, it is turned over onto a flat stone, and as many heavy stones as possible are piled upon the mass.

The weight remains until the next morning when the stones are removed, the basket slit up the sides, and the layers removed one by one. These cakes are then broken into large, relatively uniform pieces and spread on mats in the sun to dry, being turned occasionally through the heat of the day to assure good heat penetration. In the late afternoon the pieces are roughly reassembled and placed into a fresh, dusted basket, which is weighted as before and left overnight. The process is repeated the next day if further drying is needed. Great importance is attached to the thoroughness of the treading, the sufficiency of the pressing and the completeness of the drying; the quality of the drug being said to depend upon the manner in which these processes are carried out. The clue is color - if the cakes are green when the manufacture is finished the Ganja is thought to be somewhat inferior, good Ganja being a rich brown. When the cakes are fully cured they are replaced in fresh dusted baskets and stored in the headman's house under constant pressure until they can be sold to one of the circuit-riding dealers who pass through regularly throughout the year. When a dealer arrives and makes his purchase, the cakes are taken out and wrapped in sixty pound bundles covered by date-leaf mats, the trademark of Javadi Hills Ganja, which is quite highly prized throughout India.

The Pit-Planted Ganja of Mysore

Cannabis cultivators in the Mysore area of India have developed a planting technique for their gardens which yields superior Cannabis with the additional advantage that very little space is used for growing. This technique appears to be responsible for the pre-eminence of Mysore marijuana among the hemp drug products of India.

A roughly circular pit is dug twelve to eighteen inches deep in the deep red soil of the region, soil which has been well-manured over at least one season. The bottom of the pit is then dressed with hearth ashes and sweepings.

Then transplanted young Cannabis, two to three weeks old, is placed in the pit. Two techniques are used; either a single plant is placed in the center of the pit, or three to five plants are placed around the rim, which measures at least five feet in circumference. If a single plant is placed in the center of the pit, a thin layer of rotted manure or compost is spread over the bottom of the pit, and if the Cannabis is rim-planted then manure or compost is heaped generously in the pit. The pit is watered daily for the first month, once a week thereafter.

Plants which inhabit the rim grow to be an impressive seven to ten feet high, with stems as thick as a man's wrist at the base. If the single plant technique is used, the plant often reaches twelve to fourteen feet into the air, with a base as thick as a man's upper arm. In both cases the maturing plant is supported with stakes and guy-wires.

Just before the plant reaches sexual maturity, it is grasped firmly with both hands at the base and twisted vigorously, causing the stem to develop vertical cracks but taking care not to weaken the stem so much that the plant topples. This trauma is believed to stimulate resin production and to cause accelerated growth of the small leaves surrounding the flowering tops.

Traumatizing Cannabis for Higher Yield – Folk Techniques

Pruning is perhaps the most common form of traumatizing Cannabis, and is carried out in various forms in much of the Cannabis cultivating world. The principles involved seem to be fairly simple; though whether the apparent explanations of why pruning works are in fact true or are simply workable analogies is open to question.

The vegetative force of all plants seems to be directed toward the fulfillment of reproduction, and in Cannabis the secretion of the principle bearing resin is tied closely to the reproductive energies of the plant. That is, the forces which move in the plant toward the fruition of viable seeds also manifest themselves in the secretion of resin. When one interrupts the pathways by which the force of the plant is channeled into seed production, the force is redirected into greater-than-usual resin secretion.

The other major relationship with which pruning and other forms of mutilation seem to be connected is that existing between the natural form or configuration of the plant and the form which can be achieved by constricting or re-channeling its growth energies. When the plant grows in response to environmental factors without deliberate human intervention it will simply follow whatever internal patterns may exist in responding to the opportunities presented by the available nutrients and energies in its environment. The intervention of man, in effect, closes out certain natural options and forcibly presents other, limited options to the plant in fulfilling its growth pattern.

The operations which follow from the latter understanding deal largely with the stimulation of a richer, more luxuriant foliage than is normally produced by the plant growing freely in a wild or untended state. The simplest form of pruning, practiced in many parts of the world, consists of radically trimming back the branches on the lower one-third of the plant when it has attained about one-third of its growth. In general terms this means that when the plant is 2 ½ - 3 feet high, one cuts back the branches on the lower foot to foot and a half of the plant, all the way to the trunk but not flush with the trunk. A leafless stub is left, which is about six inches long. Leaving this stub promotes easy healing. The effect of this pruning is to help the plant assume a desirable pyramidal shape as its continues further growth, resulting in a greater than usual amount of its energies being directed toward the upper areas of growth where the most desirable portions of the plant for drug purposes are to be found.

A somewhat more elaborated practice of pruning, found principally in India and North Africa, consists of taking a plant which is three feet tall and not only trimming back the lower laterals somewhat (a few inches only, leaving considerable leaf) but also lopping off the top six inches to one foot of the plant. This operation produces a plant with a low profile, very bushy, with numerous flowering tops. It is an operation which proves most successful in areas which get a lot of bright, hot sun, and which are relatively dry.

The first principle mentioned above may be seen to operate in cases where the cultivator intervenes at a point in the plant's life when it is gathering its energies preparatory to flowing its major force into seed production, a point very near maturity when the seed-flower clusters are beginning to form. The mutilation takes either one of two general forms. In the first, the plant is grasped firmly at the base with both hands, as one grasps a baseball bat, and is then twisted forcibly until vertical cracks appear in the portion of the stem being attacked. The object is not to open the stem; merely to crack it sufficiently so that the plant has a substantial trauma to deal with at the point in its body which lies at the opposite pole from the seed-carrying locus. For whatever reasons, this operation produces an increased flow of resin to the flowering tops and significantly retards the production of seed.

The second method, used principally in India, consists of taking a potshard or sharp stone and inserting it into the lower stem near the ground, opening a wound in the stem. The foreign body is then left in the plant, and the wound is either bound or not, depending on local practice. This trauma then apparently redirects the energies of the plant in such a way that resin secretion to the flowering tops is significantly increased. In some places when the foreign body is inserted, a small ball of raw opium is also shoved into the stem, where it stays and is absorbed. I have also heard of the insertion of balls of aconite or datura in such cases, though there is no evidence whether or not the potency of the resin is measurably affected by such practices.

None of these practices seem to cause the death of the plant when carried out carefully. It must be the individual cultivator's decision whether or not it is right, in whatever sense one cares to use that word, to do such things.

The Traumatic Basket

Traditional cultivators have developed a variety of methods of traumatizing Cannabis over the course of the several thousand years it has been raised for drug purposes. One of the most bizarre practices ever invented to stimulate resin production is limited to a small region in the Himalayan foothills of northern India. The ordinary Cannabis plant of this area grows to a robust eight feet, and its girth is magnificent. Certain local cultivators, however, are unsatisfied with the natural configuration of the free-growing plant, and have contrived a system of binding which vastly increases resin output.

The young Cannabis is allowed to develop naturally until it is about six weeks old. Only the females (or those plants which appear to be female in potential) are utilized. A loosely-woven wicker basket, about three feet in diameter at its broadest point and with a very narrow mouth, is inverted over the young plant so that only the lower stem protrudes from the bottom. The basket is supported on wooden stakes, and the rim is lashed to the stakes with raffia or twine. The stakes are driven well into the ground, both to provide adequate support for the basket's weight and to prevent the growth of the plant from throwing off the basket.

The loose weave of the basket allows air to circulate on the inside, and allows some faint rays of sunlight to penetrate to the plant on the interior. But the plant cannot penetrate the weave, and since it can grow neither vertically nor horizontally, it must involute as it continues to grow.

The net effect of this treatment is that the fully grown plant is packed into a relatively small basket, and resembles a head of cauliflower. After several months of growth, the pale-yellow, furrowed mass of plant is released as the basket is snipped away, and falls to the ground, its atrophied stem incapable of supporting its great mass. As it lies on the grey dirt, it bears a remarkable likeness to a cerebral sphere rooted to the earth by a thin, green cord. There is ugliness and beauty in this travesty of nature-ugliness because of the aberration wrought by men in their search for a means to manipulate nature's other beings for their own ends, beauty because nature's basic drive, however expressed, is towards the survival of its living forms. There is no question that the traumatic basket treatment vastly increases resin secretion in Cannabis, though this is done at the expense of aesthetics and good karma. The basket treatment is the equivalent of force-fed, penned-in, hormone stimulated cattle raising; its motivation is quantity, not quality, and seems unlikely to attract much attention from serious, humanistic cultivators.

A Simple, Objective Test for Cannabis Potency

There are very few reliable general standards for determining the relative merits of different batches of marijuana and hashish. Even the concept of potency is not as straightforward as it may first seem, due to the subjectivity of the Cannabis experience. But if one hedges a little by defining potency as percentage of resin by weight, a simple test is available to anyone who wants to compare one type of marijuana or hashish with another.

In the case of marijuana, the stalks, seeds and any detectable foreign matter are first removed. This cleaned marijuana is then ground on a sieve having at least fifty meshes to the square inch, producing a very fine powder. Twenty grams of this fine powder is then dissolved in 4 ounces of pure grain alcohol, stirred frequently over a forty-eight hour period. The tincture is then weighed – simply weigh an empty container first, then add the liquid and weigh again. Subtracting the weight of the container gives you the weight of the tincture. The tincture is then filtered through a simple paper filter, placed in a double boiler or some similar arrangement (even on a small saucer floating on very hot water in a pan). Do NOT use an open flame like a gas stove to heat the liquid – the vapors are explosive. The tincture is heated until sufficient alcohol is evaporated to yield a syrupy liquid. This liquid is then placed, in the same container, in a warm 250° F oven until it is firm but not hard (or, if one is using sensitive lab instruments, until the weight remains constant).

The lump of almost pure resin is then weighed, and its weight is computed as a percentage of the weight of the original tincture before filtration and evaporation.

What this process does is to dissolve the resin in alcohol, then allows this resin extract to be reduced to a weighable state. Since the resin content of marijuana is so highly variable, this test provides a good comparative method for judging relative quality. With hashish, one simply ignores the sieving and straightaway dissolves twenty grams of hashish in the alcohol, and proceeds as usual with filtration, evaporation and weighing.

This test was first used by an English physician, Dr. James Evans, in his work on determining the resin content of the major strains of Marijuana (Ganja) and Hashish (Charas) on the Indian subcontinent. His work revealed a range of from 7.87% yield of alcohol extract for low quality bhang (marijuana) from Bhaglapur to a remarkable 26.47% for ganja from Kistna; and in the case of Hashish showed a low percentage yield of 18.45% on Charas from Kumann to a high of 44.55% yield for Charas from Amritsar.

Grades of Egyptian Hashish

Indigenous connoisseurs of hashish in the Mideast utilize several characteristics to grade hashish, including touch or feel, smell, appearance and color, and taste. In addition, a usual test is to take a small fragment of the hashish in question and, pressing it between two leaves of cigarette paper, set the paper aflame. The quality of smoke, and its odor, as well as the combustion characteristics give the indigenous expert a pretty good idea of the quality of the product he's dealing with.

Hashish of premier quality, known as "hashish-zahra" or "zahret-elkobch" is a brown powder in its unpressed state, perhaps sprinkled with yellow flakes; it is granular and sticky, agglutinates readily when rolled between the fingers, and when warm gives off a heavy Cannabis odor. When Zahret-el-kobch comes in cake form, it is formed in a very compact mass, is friable, and quite heavy. Microscopic examination reveals heavy concentrations of tiny hairs of the plant. There are numerous glandular fragments, most without pedicels, containing an oleo-resin which is amber in tint in fresh hashish, turning brown with age; there are also numerous crysoliths present in first quality hashish. One finds very few gross leaf or flower debris.

Second quality hashish, known as "Zahret-el-assa", is a brown-yellow powder with a clarity of color, is granular and not particularly sticky, and agglutinates with difficulty under pressure from the fingers. The odor is quite strong, but not as sensuous as that of first quality hashish. Under microscopic examination one finds numerous glandular hairs, most with the pedicels intact, and few crysoliths. There are numerous fragments of leaf epidermis and considerable number of fragments of the flower bracts.

Hashish of third grade is a yellow-green, almost dry and only just sticky, requiring the addition of water vapor to agglomerate. The caked powder is lightweight and presents a feeble odor. Under the microscope one observes some glandular hairs but mostly detached pedicels, very few crysoliths, and a large quantity of leaf and flower fragments. Upon occasion one encounters a fourth grade of hashish which is almost pure green powder, which agglutinated not at all unless significantly moist, composed almost entirely of leaf and flower fragments and very few hairs, and possessed of a very light odor.

Strep Throat? Use Dope.

(Author's note – when this section was first written in 1972-73 the idea that Cannabis could have any legitimate medical applications was consistently denied by the US anti-drug establishment – governmental, scientific and medical. That did not stop the rest of the world from pursuing the strong leads given by the historical record of Cannabis' use as a medicine.)

At the risk (gladly taken) of striking terror into the hearts of the corporate hucksters of cold and sore throat "medicines" I would like to reveal, in this section, the results of an interesting paper written in 1960 by three Czech medical researchers, entitled "Cannabis As A Medicament". So far as I've been able to discover, any attention given to the findings of these researchers has been, putting it mildly, covert.

The first part of this paper deals, as usual in such matters, with the rationale and methodology utilized in the research. I see little sense in going into detail on these points, which are of technical interest but which primarily concern themselves with the scientific validity of the results. I have checked the paper with several people who are knowledgeable about such scientific in-group concerns, and am assured that the results laid out in the paper were obtained through straightforward, valid methods of investigation, and therefore must be accepted as correct.

I'll present the results of the paper simply by quoting the authors, then add some commentary.

'The investigations were carried out with specimens of gram-positive micro-organisms - i.e., Staphylococcus pyogenes aureus - and from the gram-negative series the Escheria coli were used. The extracts produced a remarkable bactericide effect upon Staphylococcus aureus, whilst E. coli showed to be resistant. On the basis of these preliminary findings we have aimed our work in this direction. Proof could be furnished that the cannabis extracts produce a very satisfactory antibacterial effect upon the following microbes: Staphylococcus pyoenes aureus, Streptococcus alpha haemolyticus, Streptococcus beta haernolyticus, Enterococcus, Diplococcus pneumoniae, B. subtilis, B. anthracis, Corynebacterium diphtheriae and Corynebacterium cutis - i.e., all of them gram-positive micro-organism. Noteworthy is the effect upon Staphylococcus aureus strains, which are resistant to penicillin and to other antibiotics.

That was one of the peculiar properties of cannabis which was found to be most attractive. We saw the possibility of utilizing the antibiotic locally without any danger of producing resistant strains to other antibiotics administered at the same time throughout treatment. We must also remember the very good effect of substances from cannabis upon Staphylococcus aureus, particularly nowadays, when a high percentage of staphylococcus diseases offers resistance to penicillin. It is interesting that staphylococci manifesting various degrees of resistance to one or more antibiotics (erythromycin included) are sensitive to the antibiotics from cannabis in the same degree throughout. So far, we have not observed that any resistance of the staphylococcus strains to these substances would arise. The degree of the artificially produced resistance to these substances corresponds with the origin and degree of resistance to substances of the phenolic type and to other disinfectants.

The tests carried out with other micro-organisms, particularly with gram-negative strains, just as well as with fungi and yeast, gave negative results (see below). On the contrary our work evidenced the positive effect of the isolated substances upon Mycobacterium tuberculosis.

Effect of the Cannabis Indica Resin Upon Some Common Pathogenic Micro-Organisms

Investigated strain	Effect
1. Micrococcusalbus	Positive
2. Staphylococcus pyogen. aureus haemolyt. sensitive to penicillin	Positive
3. Staphylococcus pyogen. aureus haemolyt. resistant to penicillin	Positive
4. Streptococcus alpha haemolyt	Positive
5. Streptococcus beta haemolyt	Positive
6. Enterococcus	Positive
7. Diplococcus pneumoniae	Positive
8. Erysipelothrix rhusiopath	Positive
9. Sarcjna lutea	Positive
10. Corynebact. diphtheriae	Positive
11. Corynebact. cutis	Positive
12. Bac. anthracis	Positive
13. Bac. subtilis	Positive
14. Bac. mesentericus	Positive
15. Clostridium perfringens	Positive
16. Escherichia coli	Negative
17. Salmonella typhi	Negative
18. S. paratyphi B	Negative
19. Sh. Shigae (Sb. Flexneri, Sh. Kruse Sonnei)	Negative
20. Pseudomonas acruginosa	Negative
21. Proteus vulgaris	Negative
22. Mycobacterium tuberculosis	Positive

For the needs of stomatology, an aseptic dentin powder was prepared, impregnated with 2 to 5% of biologically active substances (IRC) from cannabis. This dentin powder containing IRC was successfully used for the indirect covering (in about 300 patients) and for the direct covering of the pulp (70 cases), in beginning pulpitis and irritation of the pulp. Even in cases like that we notice the obvious advantage of the antibacterial effect of the locally anesthetic action. Save in cases of massively infected pulps, Soldan did not record any failures.

Somewhat less uniform results were obtained with this preparation by Smek, who applied dentin combined with IRC or a special salve containing IRC. In uncomplicated Caries profunda, a remarkable and spontaneous effect could be achieved in 64% of the patients; in Caries profunda, with an incidental opening of the vital pulp, in 38.4% of the patients. In Pulpitis partialis, the results of this therapy were positive in 41 % of the investigated cases. The authors have, on the whole, acknowledged the anaesthetic effect of these preparations.

Very advantageous is the application of the effective substances from cannabis in otorhinolaryngology. Hubácek reports on the very good results obtained particularly after application of 1 % of an alcoholic solution of the IRC and of a dusting powder (boric acid with 2 to 5% of the IRC) in acute and chronic otitis, furunculosis of the outer part of the nostrils and of the external auditory meatus, and even in some cases of bilateral sinusitis, the latter having been treated without success with a series of punctions and penicillin irrigations. He describes an interesting case of bilateral chronic Sinusitis maxillaris, lasting for about three years and treated without success with a total of about 30 punctions. After application of our IRC preparations, one side was treated as a control with penicillin, but with negative result, and the other side with three IRC punctions and irrigations. The side treated with negative effect with penicillin was easily and successfully treated with cannabis preparations. In the same way Navrtil illustrates in his small tabe of chronic otitis a considerable improvement in 13 of a total of 18 cases. All the cases under investigation were also controlled bacteriologically. In clinical practice the very good results achieved with the preparations mentioned above - i.e., with the alcoholic solution and the dusting powder - stand in support of the good results obtained in vitro and justify the suggestion to have both these preparations made available for pharmaceutical production.

The manifold utilization of these substances particularly in the form of alcoholic solutions with glycerin has been confirmed by the results obtained after application of this preparation in obstetrics in order to prevent staphylococcic mastitis in the treatment of rhagades and fissures on the nipples of nursing women. Of great importance is the locally anesthetic component together with the antibacterial effect, particularly upon Staphylococcus aureus, which is considered to be the causing agent of the postpartum inflammation of the mamma. Heczko & Krejc{'evidenced staphylococcus in 84% of the total of 160 parturient women. It is significant that in 89% of cases the staphylococcus was resistant to penicillin, in 18% to streptomycin, and in some cases resistant to penicillin, streptomycin, aureomycin and terramycin and sensitive only to chloromycetin and to the IRC.

The publication of the results obtained from these investigations evoked a lively interest among obstetricians who up to the present have tried to find means of substitution both for the inadequate and still used gentian violet, and the local inefficacious application of some antibiotics as, for example, aureomycin, which has been recommended by some authors.

For the purpose of dermatology, a salve containing 2 % of effective substances has been prepared and found very useful in pyodermia of staphylococcic etiology, infected burns, and particularly in decubitus of immobile patients in rehabilitation centers. Of great interest was the follow-up of a physician and pathologist, who was treated with the IRC for a severe infection of the thumb of the right hand, an injury he suffered in the dissecting room. The severe condition, threatening amputation, and the absolute resistance of the micro flora to available antibiotics were overcome by substances from cannabis.

The results obtained in treatment of specific tuberculosis fistulas and published by Proem as well as the up to now unpublished results of the investigations carried out at Ivy's Hay must be considered as preliminary even though the anti-tuberculosis effect in vitro is satisfactory.

In the cases mentioned above, no extraordinary allergy of the organism to effective substances from cannabis or any particular ability of the IRC to sensitize were observed.

In conclusion we may still consider the interesting results Sirek achieved. He mentions his experiences for some years past with hemp seeds in the therapy of tuberculosis. The hemp seed was ground and extracted with milk at a temperature of 60-80°C. It represented a protein-rich moiety of the curing diet for tubercular children, in whom a remarkable improvement due to this diet was observed by the author. But the assumed anti-tuberculotic action of cannabis seeds could not be evidenced in experiments on guinea pigs. Therefore, in the cases reported by Sirek, the therapeutic effect can be only explained by the healing nutritious diet in which the specially prepared seed is of great importance.

In human therapy the best results have been obtained with the following medicaments combined with substances derived from cannabis; dusting powder together with boric acid (otitis), ointment (staphylococcus infected wounds, staphylodermia and so on), ear drops (otitis chron.), alcohol solutions with glycerin (treatment of rhagades on the nipples of nursing women - prevention of staphylococcic mastitis), aqueous emulsions (sinusitis), dentin powder with the IRC (caries). The preparations mentioned above have been already tested clinically, and will eventually be made available for production.

The high yield of effective substances (average 1.5% of the IRC in the dried drug), the considerable amount of raw material available (1.5 million hectares of cannabis plant culture in the world), and the subsequent low price both of the raw material and of the effective substances allow us to utilize the antibacterially effective substances from cannabis in veterinary medicine. Such use, which is analogical to human medicine, is comparatively wide: infected wounds (dusting powder), panaris of sheep and cattle (dusting powder), otitis in dogs (ear drops, dusting powder), mastitis in cattle, postpartum trauma, lacerated wounds and so on. Especially veterinary workers, workers concerned with cattle breeding, employees in slaughter houses, cutters and so on consider the preparations containing biologically active substances to be an important contribution to the prevention of tuberculosis, anthrax, swine erysipelas and brucellosis in various streptococcic infections of the hands and the like. The results achieved in this field, but unpublished as yet, justify the greatest optimism.

In view of the results obtained with antibacterially effective substances isolated from cannabis, it may be concluded that they are superior and have numerous advantages as antibiotics."

What the authors of this paper have demonstrated is that preparations of Cannabis can be amazingly effective in the treatment of a wide range of medical problems. The meaning of this information is manyfold. First, it seems, anyone who is afflicted with any of the problems outlined in this paper would be well advised to see to it that any doctor chosen to deal with the problem is made aware of these options. And, of course, there are substantial possibilities for treating yourself with Cannabis in the absence of flexible and well-informed medical assistance.

Also of great interest to me is the fact that many of the properties described as emanating from Cannabis in this paper have been known in the traditional medical systems of the world for thousands of years in some cases. The authors of the paper are, of course, aware of this fact, and devote a section in the beginning of their report to a survey of some of the traditional medical practices relevant to their present research, though they by no means cover the range of information available.

Cannabis In Folk Medicine Traditions

NB Please note that this section was written in 1973-4, long before the 'Medical Marijuana' movement began. However, its interesting how many of these traditional uses of Cannabis as a medicine have much more recently been 'discovered' by both the Western medical establishment and the Medical Marijuana movement.

Cannabis as a medicine has a long history in the treatment of both human and animal diseases and disorders, and is particularly well integrated into both the Ayurvedic system of Hindu treatment in India and the various systems of Arabic medicine, known in India as Unani Tibbi. Cannabis preparations are also a part of Arab medical systems in Iran, and in various systems extant throughout the Arab world; the two primary works concerning the use of Cannabis in such systems are the Firdo usul-Hikmat, and the Mujardat Qucinan, the first Arabic, and the second Persian. The primary Ayurvedic texts with reference to the use of Cannabis are the Susruta, the Rajanirghanta (300 A.D., again published 1500 A.D.), the Sarangadhara Samhita (c.800 A.D.), the Dhurtasarnagarna (c.1500 A. D.), and the Bhavaprakash (c.1600 A. D.).

The properties of Cannabis as described in Ayurvedic medicine include that of loosening and promotion of release of phlegm; excitation of the flow of bile; stimulation of the digestive fires; promotion of internal heat; stimulation of the appetite; promotion of taste; and stimulation of speech; it also promotes bowel retention, stimulates happiness, and acts as an hypnotic. It is also utilized to stimulate the libido, and is known to cause mental confusion and intoxication. Its names in Ayurvedic medicine signify that Cannabis causes garrulousness, mental confusion, vacillation and drowsiness, and induces states in which one feels unconquerable, capable of penetrating and integrating the three worlds, and in which one feels intense pleasure and elation of the spirit. (No wonder this shit is illegal – imagine – intense pleasure and elation of spirit. Wouldn't want folks feeling that way. No sirreee.)

Also of great interest to me is the fact that many of the properties described as emanating from Cannabis in this paper have been known in the traditional medical systems of the world for thousands of years in some cases. The authors of the paper are, of course, aware of this fact, and devote a section in the beginning of their report to a survey of some of the traditional medical practices relevant to their present research, though they by no means cover the range of information available. Let's look at that phenomenon, the traditional uses of Cannabis in Folk medicine. I'll offer the reader a compendium of what I've found in a number of diverse sources, without trying to screen the information for validity, first because I'm not in any position to judge the truth of such matters, and second because it is all fascinating information, whether true or not.

Other recognized uses of Cannabis in Ayurvedic traditions include its application as a stimulating, aphrodisiacal tonic, as a treatment for bloody diarrhea or dysentery with fever, in cases of renal colic, dysmenorrhoea, dyspepsia, bronchitis, fever and piles (hemorrhoids). It is also recognized as useful in various preparations as a specific remedy for asthma, coughs, debility, acidity, gout, abdominal swellings, tumors or general complaints.

In Muslim medicine, the properties of Cannabis known to be useful min the treatment of human complaints include its tonic qualities, its property of inducing nervous excitement, its function as an aphrodisiac, its function of binding the bowels, its ability to cleanse body impurities and to promote dryness of the mouth, throat and lungs, and its value as an antiphlegmatic. It is also prescribed in various preparations for treatment of asthma, diarrhea, problems of nocturnal emission, sexual impotency, insomnia, irritability, rheumatic pains, neuritis and neuralgia, and poor appetite.

Illiterate people in rural India and elsewhere in the near east have discovered many folk remedies based on Cannabis, no doubt evolving from the ancient wisdom of the Ayurvedic medical texts passed down through verbal traditions. For example, crushed fresh Cannabis leaves are rubbed into the scalp for treating both lice and dandruff. Cannabis beverages are used to provide symptomatic relief from gonorrhea. It is also used as an antispasmodic in severe asthma, hay fever and bronchitis, in which cases it is often smoked in a mixture with tobacco. This approach makes good sense. The combination of Cannabis and tobacco acts as a pulmonary sedative, and since the tradition is to hold Cannabis smoke in the lungs for as long as possible the sedative properties of both Cannabis and tobacco are given time to take effect whereas a puff or two of quickly exhaled tobacco would not be as effective. It also seems reasonable to assume that the contribution of Cannabis to the sufferer's morale plays no small part in the treatment.

The usefulness of Cannabis, particularly hashish preparations, in the case of dental problems noted in the preceding Czech research paper is well-known in the areas which are encompassed by Ayurvedic and Tibbi medicine. Again, not only does the hashish have a sedative and antiseptic effect on the painful tooth, but the juices trickling down into the insides of the sufferer cannot do any harm.

Hashish is extensively used to combat insomnia, for which there are few effective cures available in rural and remote areas of the world, and for which opium is known to be, if not ineffective in producing sleep, then at least contributory to other subsequent sleep problems.

While it may astound many American heads accustomed to giving in to the urges of the blind munchies, Cannabis is used extensively in spiritual fasting in many parts of India. It is also used, as smokers well know, to promote deepened thought and to render clear, matters of complex spiritual insight. It is also used by craftsmen whose work requires intense concentration - jewelers, watchmakers, painters and illuminators of religious manuscripts, to enumerate a few.

The antibacterial action of Cannabis, discovered and elaborated upon in the Czech paper, is well-known in the Near and Far East. The use of Cannabis leaves in a poultice, often rendered soft and warm through the use of heated castor oil, is common in cases of external infection and inflammation. Such poultices are commonly used in inflammations of the eyes, ears, nose and mouth, and in cases of swollen joints and abdominal complaint. Powdered ganja or hashish enjoys a superb reputation in checking superficial bleeding, and is used extensively in tincture form for the treatment of uterine bleeding from childbirth. In some places it is the ash of Cannabis which is thought most useful in the treatment of sores, burns and skin ulcerations.

Cannabis has for many years enjoyed a sterling reputation as an anesthetic, though it is rarely used when opium is available. It is frequently used in matters such as tooth extraction and minor operations of that sort, and has also been found useful in cases of protracted labor pains, cramps, dysmenorrhoea, neuralgia, and general abdominal pains.

Then, too, there is general agreement among the hard working people of the Far and Near Eastern countries as to the beneficial effects of Cannabis concoctions in giving staying power under severe exertion or exposure, and to alleviate fatigue. Cannabis is used regularly by such diverse groups as gymnasts, wrestlers, musicians, porters, divers and runners. Nineteenth century literature often notes the use of Cannabis by watchmen, blacksmiths, miners, coolies and fisherman particularly. Perhaps the most inclusive observation as to why Cannabis is considered so useful by so many people in such .diverse circumstances was recorded by the Indian Hemp Drugs Commission, which noted that, "The drugs are said to be cheering and uplifting in their effect, and are prized by many on this account."

In another report on British colonial affairs, a doctor reported that there is a large body of evidence showing "that hemp drugs, both as smoked and drunk, are used as a ferbifuge or preventative of the diseases common in malarial tracts or arising from the use of bad water. The evidence is considerable. Laborers in marshy or vile areas, cultivators of wet lands of the far interior, jungle tribes, and those who have to work or reside in jungle tracts are among those who use the drugs for these purposes. It is impossible to shut the eyes to evidence, which one often comes upon unexpectedly, showing that respectable and intelligent people going on duty to such tracts, and sepoys sent on foreign service or garrisoning comparatively unhealthy districts, often take to these drugs for therapeutic purposes."

In a comment on such evidence, one British civil servant, in an excess of zeal for such a functionary, wrote: "As some opium smokers attribute all manner of good effects to opium, liquor drinkers to alcohol, and tobacco smokers to tobacco, so do consumers of hemp drugs praise their choice. It is, no doubt, true that there is a tendency to find excuse for an unnecessary indulgence. But the proven medical uses of hemp drugs lend at least some measure of support to the belief among users that some beneficial effects do follow from moderate use."

Cannabis is often recommended for ailments afflicting the more exotic part of the human body. In some cases of swollen testicles, a warm poultice prepared from marijuana leaves and oil is applied to the tender area, and bound in place with a warmed, fresh fig leaf (which throws an interesting light on those old Fig leaf-Garden of Eden images). A poultice of marijuana is said to work wonders with hemorrhoids. An alternative to the poultice method for hemorrhoid relief is for the sufferer to dig a small pit, placing therein several hot coals and a little wad of good quality marijuana. Dropping drawers, the hopeful patient then squats over the ascending fumes and his troubles, thus soothingly fumigated, are said to recede.

As noted by the Czech researchers, Cannabis is potentially quite useful in Veterinary medicine, as has been long recognized in the Near and Far East. A very common use of Cannabis is to produce conditions in working animals, to relieve fatigue and increase staying power, to make elephants stout of heart and oxen fleet of foot. It is considered useful in disinfecting stables and folds, and in this connection is simply burned in great heaps in the area to be disinfected. The smoke is said to drive out or kill the pests which are the object of concern. When valuable animals suffer from respiratory troubles, they are put in an enclosed space, and a pound or two of Cannabis is burned. In cases of colic or other similar bowel complaints, a large "pill" is made by mixing flowering tops together with sugar and grain and fed to the animal. Ganja which is heavy with seeds is useful in worming, and is also thought useful in rinderpest. Bhang is often given to cattle which have problems of decreasing milk supply, and to female animals which are about to be mated. Bhang or ganja is also used extensively in animal diarrhea, particularly in the case of elephants which are prone to this trouble during monsoon season. One must assume that this application, in particular, demonstrates that there is a pragmatic efficacy to the use of Cannabis - an elephant keeper would hardly miss the point if the remedy were not effective.

As a bit of an aside, a point occurs to me with reference to these traditional uses of Cannabis in veterinary medicine. I offer it gratis to anyone who would like to try it out.

Cannabis is a simple drug with few side-effects, and is apparently useful for a wide variety of animal ailments, many of which are treated in the veterinary medicine systems of this country with hormones, antibiotics and all manner of complicated and devious substances.

The poultry industry in America is huge, and there are few countries in the world which do not rely on chickens for a large proportion of their meat supply. One of the foremost problems of chicken raisers is that chickens will often go off their feed, particularly when they are cooped up by the thousands in small spaces. When this happens in this country, the chicken's feed is pumped full of hormones which act to fatten the bird whether or not it eats well. In many other countries, the problem of chicken appetite is treated with a generous dose of hemp seed; in fact, hemp seed is used regularly and no such problem occurs. Hemp seed not only fattens chickens, it is used to increase egg production in hens, and is thought to be quite beneficial in such matters. Hemp seed is, by the way, a monopoly of the bird seed industry in America, and was specifically exempted from the Marijuana Tax Stamp Act of 1937 as a result of frantic lobbying by the bird seed industry, which recognized its merits. But the use of potent hemp seed has never caught on among chicken farmers, probably because marijuana was illegal and thus no ready supply of seeds existed. And, too, the hemp seed which is legal is sterilized and contains no resin; imagine the results if chickens were fed on seed which had been shaken loose from flowering tops of a ripe female, seed which retained even the tiniest bit of the amber gum so beloved of smokers. My experience with chickens is limited, but I would not be the least surprised to find that a mellow chicken laid more eggs, put on more weight, and tasted better. Another problem of chicken raisers which might be solved by the sticky seed treatment is that the birds frequently attack each other, particularly when they are kept in close quarters. There is a high mortality rate among chickens in mass breeding pens. It's fair to speculate that a flock of semi-stoned chickens would be far less likely to peck and bite each other than would a flock of neurotic, pressured birds.

Cannabis As A Potent Old Age Treatment

The banners of organized medicine are dropping a bit these days, so many of its cherished principles are being seriously undermined by knowledge which is not new, which has been available for a long time, but which has been ignored or passed off with professional contempt. Organized medicine is particularly guilty of having gone along with the marijuana polemic of the government narcotics bureaus, and has only recently begun qualifying its condemnation of marijuana as a useless, dangerous drug.

Medicine has backed off from outright nay-saying, and is now taking the position that "Marijuana has no recognized medical use." The key word, of course, is recognized. Some such qualifier is invariably used when the issue of marijuana's place in the medical heavens is raised.

In fact, marijuana is a very useful drug. In time, its usefulness will be found to extend even to some of those areas most jealously guarded by the AMA. However, before most of marijuana's useful applications can be formally admitted to practice, medical imagination will have to be stimulated.

Marijuana's most useful application stems from its most generally recognized characteristic -it is a superior euphoriant. In this sense, it is a tool, a tool of joy. Euphoria is most frequently thought of as a free-floating state, essentially a passive, non-thinking release from whatever depressive devils afflict a person in his normal, unstoned states of consciousness. What is required is a shift in attitude; euphoria as a tool, the application of euphoria to a reworking of the normal states which are being escaped. If euphoria is conceived of as an escape, as a release from the problems of normal states of consciousness, then it is made into a temporary and essentially useless interlude between periods of strain and imbalance. The neurosis of normality lies behind and before the smoker; he will return to what he has only fleetingly left behind. If, on the other hand, the euphoric state is viewed and used as an elevated workbench, a gaining of perspective from which the problems of the normal state may be seen from another level, then it becomes possible to draw strength and knowledge from the experience which can be applied to the normal state experience even after the euphoria has passed.

The marijuana experience can be integrating or disintegrating; it depends largely upon the wisdom of the person using the drug. One of the remarkable characteristics of the marijuana phenomenon in this country is that so many people seem to use marijuana as a tool without ever having articulated this aspect of the drug's usefulness for themselves. It seems as though marijuana falls quite naturally into this configuration for relatively healthy, stable people whether or not they develop a conception of it in this way. Certainly marijuana is a better tool for dealing with normal-state problems and neurosis than are the other euphoric drugs in common use in this society. If organized medicine were ever to explore this aspect of marijuana, and were able to apply it in a humanistic rather than in a clinical setting, it would have discovered a powerful force for the relief of some of the most common human anguish.

I believe that the elderly would be prime beneficiaries of a wise policy of marijuana administration, particularly those legions of old people who are benignly but firmly imprisoned in rest homes, nursing homes other such golden-age purgatories. Life in these places is by and large tasteless, hopeless, deaf and dumb, colorless and without happiness. As people grow old, their sensory pathways deteriorate. Much of the deterioration comes from disuse; in most places where old people are put away, no effort is made to stimulate them. On the contrary, they are generally sedated, on the barbaric theory that if they don't realize what they're missing, they won't care and, incidentally, won't cause trouble with their complaints.

Marijuana would turn old people on once again. Food would become tasty and desirable; the blind munchies are no respecter of age. Music appreciation could become a new experience, even for those who had never before turned on to music and sound. Form and color senses would be stimulated, and old people would be able to spend hours absorbed in the sensual experiences of red and green and blue. New forms of human relationships could be explored; conversation would be generated by the private thoughts of old people turned on once again to the presence of others with whom such thoughts could be shared. Thought and contemplation would be stimulated at a period of human life when such pursuits are most rewarding of all, when the last great experience lies immediately ahead.

It would not be likely, of course, that the people who run these institutions would take any great part in the process of turning old people on. Many, if not all of the people who run rest homes and the like are motivated by the money to be made rather than by love of their charges. The answer seems to lie in the community of heads, many of whom daily seek answers to a life which is confusing enough even when twenty or thirty years of experience has been digested and absorbed. Imagine what could be learned from old people if we could smoke together. Think of what could be said, and what could be taught in ways which by their nature are best unspoken. Given the opportunity, many heads would seek out old people, would go to the institutions and seek out the elderly, and would learn from them many things which otherwise would not be possible.

SECTION TWO: THE CULTIVATION AND USE OF COCA

Introduction

The Inca were chewing Coca leaves and building a great Andean empire and civilization while European man was still in his hovels chewing on bones. By all available accounts, Peru seems to be the place of genesis for Erythroxylon Coca, though it had already diffused far from the valleys of the Incas long before the plundering Spanish swept through the high streets of Incan cities.

E. Coca thrives over a wide geographical range, but has fairly specific environmental preferences. In Bolivia, its growth is limited to the Eastern Cordillera, the high, temperate foothills of the great Andean spine. In the Argentine, Coca groves nestle up against the southern tailings of the Andes, preferring the low temperate valleys to the warmer plains of grass and scrub brush. In Colombia there are extensive Coca plantings in the South and West, where the valleys mirror growing conditions in Peru, across the high ranges, and in Brazil there once were extensive plantings along her westernmost border above the Amazon headwaters, though these plantations are considerably diminished and mostly gone to the wild state today.

During the 19th Century there were numerous attempts made to establish Coca plantations in Jamaica, Puerto Rico, Mexico, Algeria, and California and these, while failing to show significant commercial potential for that time, were nevertheless successful enough to give encouragement to anyone who seeks to initiate a small-scale personal project today.

The 19th Century also saw significant efforts at commercial-scale cocaine production in the Far East. In 1870 a consortium of British origin, using specimens obtained originally from Peru by the Botanical staff of Kew Gardens opened a Coca plantation in Ceylon. The plants did remarkably well in the high, moist, temperate valleys of central Ceylon, and were in turn used to seed several equally successful plantations in the Presidency of Madras in India. In the Western mountains of Madras there are a series of parallel valleys lying between 1000 and 4000 feet elevation, and perfectly suited for rampant Coca growth. Despite the success experienced by the British, however, the Cocaine produced in Ceylon and Madras was not sufficiently high in alkaloid content to make it competitive with production in Java.

In 1878 a Belgian firm, using stock from the botanical gardens at Beitenzorg founded a plantation in Java, and by 1883 they harvested their first crop of young leaves. Within three more years the Belgians had the largest facility for the production of high grade Cocaine in existence outside of Peru, and their product was eventually to prove out at a higher quality than even the South American leaves.

Various other Coca enterprises were founded in the far east during this period - notably in Madura, Sumatra and Queensland, but none proved as enduring as the plantations of Java, though today one may still find wild, escaped Coca plants in these areas, along with a good deal of clandestine cultivation.

In Search of the Elusive Coca Plant

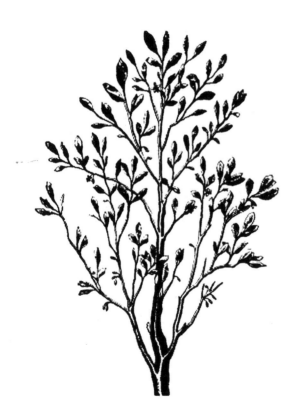

The Coca tree is easily recognized and, if one finds one's self travelling through the hinterlands of South America or the Far East, or perhaps even Puerto Rico, Algeria or Lebanon, one might do well to keep an eye out for the beauty of Erythroxylon Coca.

It is a delicate little tree which can upon occasion reach heights of 15-18', but which in fact rarely exceeds 8' in height. Its root system is a large clump of fine rootlets, each terminated by a little tuft of gossamer. The trunk is wrapped in a heavily scored bark, frequently called home by an impressive array of lichen, mushrooms and tiny critters. The lower branches coming off this trunk are few in number; they are alternate on either side, protrude at right angles to the trunk, are occasionally forked and are lightly garnished with leaves.

The young branches higher on the tree are a pale fern grey. As these branches age they will shift color through a bright green, to a green verging on yellow, and will vary gradually, in the course of ten years or so, then return to the original grey part of the spectrum, finally matching the trunk in color.

The leaves are alternate, and are arranged so that their upper faces are always aligned in an orientation with the summit of the tree. The form of the leaves is generally oblong, smooth at the tip and base with a short stem, shaped very much like the leaves of the orange tree. There is a marked darkening aureole effect along the central vein of the leaf. At the base of each leaf one finds a pair of green-brown stipules which are joined together in a roughly triangular shape, and these persist after the leaf has fallen away, leaving a scaly patch for the wound created by the separation.

The flower buds of Coca nestle against the pitted base of the leaves, and can occur either singly or in groups of as much as ten. The bud is ovoid and with each new push of leaves after a harvest these little clusters - those remaining, that is, on the un-harvested parts of the tree, burst almost immediately into flower. The floral plan is pentametrical, with the petals rising from the base of the bud as a spiral curve with logarythmic proportions.

The flowers are small, delicate and creamy white, and breathe out a faint, sweet aura. The calix is green, and is composed of five sepals, each smooth and pointed, springing from a common base and grandly spread at the summit. The corolla has also five petals, cream-colored, alternate with the sepals, and with the shape of an elongated oval with a faint central nerve showing more on the upper face than on the lower. The corolla falls away immediately after the bloom is full, leaving a naked pistle.

The stamens number ten, and are pale green filaments of varying length, with the longer ones near the sepals, and the shorter near the flower corolla. The stamens rise from the base of the pistle, from inside a small cusp which serves as the nestling place of the ovaries. The ovum are carried within three little wedge-shaped cups within the ovary; after fertilization, all but one of these egg chambers atrophies so that the plant's vital forces can flow undivided into reproduction.

The new fruit of Coca is pulpy and mucilaginous, a pale green ovoid about a quarter of an inch long, with vestiges of flower adhering to its base. The color of the fruit changes with maturity to a brilliant red, and after fallen and dry it assumes a deep blue-black hue. The seed, only slightly smaller than the dry fruit, is pointed at either end, and is divided longitudinally into six lobes. It is a smooth, pale flesh color. The seed husk is very thin, and the kernel is easily exposed as a hard, white little egg-shaped body.

Scientific & Personal Observations on Medicinal Coca

EACH race has its fashions and fancies in natural intoxicants. The Indian munches the betel; the Chinaman woos with passion the brutalizing intoxication of opium; the European occupies his idle hours or employs his leisure ones in smoking, chewing or snuffing tobacco. Guided by a happier instinct, the native of South America has adopted Coca. When young, he robs his father of it; later on, he devotes his first savings to its purchase. Without it he would fear vertigo on the summit of the Andes, and weaken at his severe labor in the mines. It is with him everywhere; even in his sleep he keeps his precious quid in his mouth.

But should Coca be regarded merely as a masticatory? And must we accept as irrevocable the decision of certain therapeutists: "Cocaine, worthless; Coca, superfluous drug"?

For several years laryngologists such as Fauvel, of France; Morell, Mackenzie and Lennox Browne, of England; and Elsberg, of America, had undertaken the defense of Coca. Under such patronage Coca and its preparations were not slow in becoming popular.

Charles Fauvel was the first to make use of it as a general tonic, having a special action on the larynx; and to make known its anesthetic and analgesic qualities.

Coca was further recommended, as it were empirically, against stomatitis, gingivitis, gastric disturbances, and phthisis "Elèments de thèrapeutique el de pharmacologie" (Rabuteau).

Although striking effects were obtained from this valuable medicine, its full worth was yet unknown and there was diversity of opinion as to its mode of action, until the communications of Kóller, of Vienna, "On Coca and Cocaine", appeared in 1884.

These interesting publications led to such general discussion among medical men, that nearly every one eagerly followed the work, and watched the splendid results obtained by the Viennese physician (now Professor of Ophthalmology in New York Polyclinic).

It is found that studies made of the active principles of Coca have entirely corroborated our previsions, and probably no subject has received greater attention than have the virtues of this little Peruvian shrub, formerly looked upon in Europe with so much indifference.

The scientific study of the principles of Coca maybe considered as completed; and we believe that the time has arrived in which to summarize data regarding this therapeutic agent, so that the employment of our preparations may be based on positive clinical experience.

It is to empiricism and that alone that we owe our first knowledge of the physiological action of Coca. There is nothing surprising in that, for empiricism is nothing more, in reality, than unconscious observation.

The Indians, who from time immemorial consumed so great a quantity of Coca leaves, did not do so merely from religious sentiment which deified the leaves of Coca, they well knew that they would derive great benefit from its use: they knew it only too well, since it is to that cause that we must attribute the legendary accounts given by the first authors' who wrote on Coca.

This veneration for Coca arose, as we have seen, from its wonderful qualities. There are indeed, in this direction, some truly extraordinary accounts which should not be dismissed without notice, as they are given in good faith. Unanue, of Lima, relates that at the siege of La Paz, Bolivia, in 1781, only those inhabitants who had taken Coca were able to endure hunger and fatigue. Nearly all of the soldiers perished, deprived, as they were of food and overcome by forced marches, except those who had taken the precaution to provide themselves with Coca leaves.

It must not be believed that this prolonged fast, sustained by the use of Coca, wastes the strength and is injurious to the health. The Indians who pass an entire day without eating, notwithstanding the hardship of marches, content themselves with chewing Coca leaves, and eat heartily in the evening.

"The Indians who accompanied me on my voyage," says Weddel, "chewed Coca leaves all day, neither drinking, eating nor showing any signs of fatigue. But at evening they their stomachs like men who were completely famished, and I can assure you that I have sometimes seen devour at one meal more aliment than I could have consumed in two days." We will see, further on, that it is in exciting the nervous and muscular functions, in and partly in producing a soothing effect on the mucous membrane of the stomach, that Coca produces these wonderful results in the conservation of energy without the tortures of hunger, notwithstanding the deprivation of aliment.

In 1859 Niemann discovered the active principle of the leaves of Coca, to which he gave the name- of Cocaine, though, in fact, the of this alkaloid should be attributed to Gardeke, who had separated it in 1855 under the name of *Erythroxyline.*

The work of Demarle appeared that same year, entitled "The Coca of Peru", in which he pointed out certain properties attributed by him to the alkaloid that the of the plant and which he studied. He remarked, among other things, on the dilatation of the pupils, which he had noticed in his own case after taking a dose of Coca, as well as the absence of taste for a length of time after crushing some leaves with his teeth and holding them in the mouth.

Chewing a dose of twenty grams of Coca leaves produces an increase of the heart-beat, increasing pulse, and finally a rise in temperature. Mantegazza observed on himself that, under the influence of such a dose, his pulse increased from 65 to 124.

Moreno, who repeated the same experiment, obtained results. The respiration is increased in the same proportion as the circulation. The same dose, or even a weaker one, produces a remarkably stimulating effect on the nervous system. It is from this stimulating effect that Coca makes one more active and vigorous and enables those to accomplish more work who, without it, would soon be overcome with fatigue.

The use of larger doses (60 grams of leaves for example) has caused intoxication, accompanied by sensation of happiness, makes everything appear under a favorable aspect.

Mantegazza, who experienced this intoxication, describes his sensations in an animated style, which recalls that of the Oriental legends: "Borne on the wings of two Coca leaves, I flew about in the spaces of 77,438 worlds, one more splendid than I prefer a life of ten years with Coca to one of a hundred thousand without it. It to me that I was rated from the whole world, and I beheld the strangest images, most beautiful in color and in that can be imagined."

Dr. Gazeau, in 1870, studied the stimulating effect of Coca on nutrition, and found that it increased the pulse and assisted digestion, increased urinary excretion, and strengthened the nervous This author at the conclusion states clearly that Coca prolongs life, and advises its use, locally for stomatitis, gingivitis, ulceration, and generally for painful and difficult gastric disturbances, and also for obesity.

It was Charles Fauvel who first described the anesthesia of Coca on the pharyngeal mucous membrane. Thanks to this circumstance, he has been able to derive much benefit from the use of Coca in granular pharyngitis which is generally unaffected any other kind of treatment.

Fauvel further showed that the stimulating effect which Coca exercises on all the muscles, appears to manifest itself specially on all the muscles of the larynx. Hence his apt qualification of the drug, "a tensor *par excellence* of the vocal cords." In 1880, Von Arep published the results of his physiological researches with Cocaine. He spoke of its double effect on the nervous extremities and on the central nervous "We approach, on leaving this the scientific era, that is to say, that of physiological experiments. All the having been made with Cocaine, we shall speak of it in the next chapter, which will be devoted exclusively to the study of this alkaloid. Before closing, we will mention that it has been claimed frequently that Coca was aphrodisiac. The fact that the 'Peruvian Venus' was represented as holding her hand a leaf Coca, was suggested as a proof in support of this opinion. Dr. Unanue speaks of "certain men eighty years of age and over, and yet capable of such prowess as young men in the prime of life would be proud of."

Here let us add that the so-called unhappy consequences of the abuse of Coca are really much more rare than those produced even by tobacco, alcohol or opium. The constant use of reasonable doses of Coca appears to produce a diametrically opposite effect, and the authors, who have seen large numbers of Coca consumers, report cases of astonishing longevity the Indian coqueros (Tschudy, Campbell, Mantegazza, Unanue). They add that these instances are far from being exceptional.

Mother Coca Presents The Divine Gift To The Old World

The 1800s saw heated debate regarding the medicinal properties of Coca, with credible and incredible testimony from all sides. In his book "A New Form of Nervous Disease", a Dr. XXXX recounts his experience with hundreds of patients with a wide range of nervous system problems. While contemporary medicine has invented hundreds of compounds to address these same problems, one has to wonder if much progress has really been made, and whether allowing people to grow their own Coca plants for self-medication isn't the most enlightened policy. Here are some of Dr. XXXX's comments on the topic, as well as a few of his patients in their own words:

With the exception, perhaps, of the notorious Digitalis, no drug has so baffled all investigations into its effects upon the healthy human system. Some experimenters deride and decry its virtues as the merest fiction, while others are positive and enthusiastic as to its effects. Setting aside the fact that some persons are much more susceptible others to substances of this class, I think we shall find abundant reason this wide difference opinion hereafter.

According to the National Dispensatory, very large doses have produced convulsions in animals. Smaller quantities give hyperesthesia and dilatation of the pupils. A diminution of movement is apparent, seeming to be caused by a loss of coordinating power. Bennett claims that on man cocaine, and the alkaloids of tea, coffee, guarana, and cocoa have identical effects. During five days' use of Coca, Ott found the solid elements of the urine diminished, while the weight of the body slight increased. During his experiments the urine contained oxalate of lime. Gazeau found it to increase the urea and diminish weight. His opinion is that its power consists in its sustained excitation of vital force, added to which is an anesthetic power which lessens the sense of fatigue and hunger - an opinion that has very little foundation in physiology or toxicology as at present understood.

An excellent account of the Coca is found in a work entitled" Voyage dans le Nord de Bolivie," by Dr. H. A. Weddell, Paris, 1853. This author denies the existence of the injurious effects which some travelers have attributed to its prolonged use. After careful daily observation of his Indians who chewed it in excess, he could not discover that it injured them. He says its effects to be gentle and sustained: that it seemed rather to affect the whole system than the brain alone; and, although without any true nutritive powers, it afforded support which differs from that of an other stimuli in not being transient leaving no reactionary depression. The following is an abstract of the experiments of Dr. Christison.

His first trial was in 1870. Two of his students had been thoroughly tired by a walk of sixteen miles, returning to dinner in the evening, having eaten no food since Nine AM. They then, instead of food, drank two drachms of Coca in infusion. Soon a sense of fatigue and hunger vanished, and they took another walk of an hour's duration with ease and pleasure. They returned with good appetite, felt alert during the evening, slept well all night and woke in the morning refreshed and active.

In May, 1870, Dr. Christison himself walked fifteen miles, in stages, with intervals of half an hour's rest, and without food or drink after 8:30 A. M. He found the task excessively wearisome, and was as effectually tired out as ever in his life. The amount of urinary solids was taken two hours. He found a decided increase during the forenoon, which diminished during rest after dinner. His pulse when at rest was 62. When he returned from his walk it was 110. Two hours afterward 90. He could do no mental labor in the evening and woke in the morning wearied and lazy.

Four days after the last trial, and with the same dietary, he walked sixteen miles, in stages of four and six miles, taking, as before, half hour intervals of rest. During the second rest he chewed eighty grains of Coca. On completing previous ten miles he was fagged enough to anticipate with dread the remaining six. He felt no effect from the Coca until he stepped out of doors, when, to his surprise, all weariness fled and he found that he could walk with ease and elasticity. Accomplished the six miles without difficulty, and ran up two flights of stairs to his room, taking two steps at once. The pulse 90, and two hours after, 72. The urinary solids were the same as when not under the influence of Coca.

Upon his return and before dinner he felt neither hunger nor thirst, but ate well. In the evening was alert and not drowsy: slept well, and woke in the morning refreshed and free from fatigue. On September 15th he ascended a mountain about 3000 feet above the road. It required two and a half hours to reach the summit, and he was so much fatigued that it required much determination to get over the last three hundred feet. His companions ate lunch, but he chewed instead two thirds of a drachm of Coca. He experienced no fatigue while going down, and after returning home felt no hunger, nor thirst, nor weariness. At P.M. he took dinner, and felt lively and well during the evening. He had taken no food nor drink from A. M. till P. M., and had chewed in all eighty of Coca. Eight days ward he repeated the same experiment' with even more complete His son also obtained quite equal effects.

Not all agree that Coca is an antidote to hunger and stress. In a letter to the London *Lancet* (1876) the writer, a physician, thus expresses himself:

"… much has been said regarding my use of the South American Coca that I deem it a duty to correct an impression which is erroneous. During my first trial in London, on the 9th of February, while walking from my sixty-fifth to my seventy-fifth mile, I chewed the Coca leaves freely, acting under the advice of my medical adviser in America. . I found they did not have the effect expected, that is, they would not keep me awake nor in the least stimulate efforts. But, on the contrary, they acted as an opiate, and forced me to sleep, which was mainly the cause of my absence from the track for forty-five minutes the seventy-fifth mile. Previous experience in America, taken with this, leads me to the belief that, far from being an assistance in any trial of physical endurance, the use of these leaves quantity would- prove a great detriment."

In direct contrast with this let us place a quotation from the traveler Von Tschudi:

"A cholo of Huari, named Batan Huamang, was employed by me in laborious digging. During the days and nights he was in my service he never tasted any food, and took only two hours sleep each night. But, at of about three hours he regularly chewed about half an ounce of Coca leaves and always kept some in his mouth. I was constantly beside him, and therefore had the opportunity of closely observing him. The work for which I had engaged him being finished, he accompanied me on a two days' journey of twenty-three leagues. Though on foot, he kept pace with my mule, and halted only for a visit with his popero. On leaving me he declared that he would willingly engage himself for the same amount of work, and go through it without food if I would but allow him a sufficient supply of Coca. The village priest told me that this man was sixty-two years of age, and that he had never known him to be sick in his life. "

Illustrating the power of Coca in preventing breathlessness, the same writer says: "When I was in the Puna, at the height of 14,000 feet above level of the sea, I always drank before going out to hunt a strong infusion of the Coca. I could then, the whole day, climb the heights, and follow the swift footed wild animals without experiencing any greater difficulty of breathing than I should have felt at the sea. However, I always felt a sense of great satiety after taking the infusion, and did not have a for my next meal until after the time at which I usually took it."

Much has been written by various observers, especially by Poppig, of the baneful effects of Coca chewing. It is quite evident, however, that they, like some *soi-disant* philosophers who refer every recent disease to the influence of vaccination or to the use of tobacco, have looked through strongly prejudiced eyes and attributed all the imperfections and disorders, both of mind and body, which they have found among the half savage and debased Peruvian Indians, to Coca alone. In regard to this point Von Tschudi, as the sum of his inquiries, says: "Setting aside all extravagant and visionary notions, I am clearly of opinion that the moderate use of Coca is not merely innocuous, but that it may be even very conducive to health. In support of these conclusions, I may refer to the numerous examples of longevity among those who almost from boyhood have been in the habit of masticating Coca three times a day. Stories are not infrequent of Indians attaining the age of one hundred and thirty years, who must, in the course of their lives, have chewed not less than 2700 pounds of the leaf, and yet retained perfect health."

Supporting evidence was published by Dr. Mantegazza in the *Amtali di Med., 1859*. Dr. Mantegazza resided and practiced in South America for some years, and was conversant with the use of Coca in every form, both as employed by the natives and prescribed by himself. His account of its properties is most eulogistic. He noted that it stimulates the stomach and aids digestion. In large doses it may produce fever and slight constipation. In medium one to two drachms-it stimulates the nervous system and increases muscular power, rendering it independent of external influences, and inducing a happy state of tranquility which it confers without impairment of strength. He recommends a warm infusion of the leaves after meals for weak digestion, or the effects of intemperance. He himself used it for two years without injurious effects, and, though usually unable to work after dinner without headache and indigestion, these symptoms did not occur when he used the Coca. He advises the infusion for acidity and flatulence, and states that its use by the miners renders their teeth white, though other authorities state the exact reverse. It is a useful tonic in nervous prostration, hysteria, and melancholy, but dangerous in congestion. He considers it better than opium in mental affections, and believes that, in sustaining nervous force, it is superior to all known agents. He cites eighteen cases of disease of varied character in which it proved curative.

The author of this paper first became acquainted with the Coca in the year 1865. In May of the following year I obtained my first specimen from Peru. It was a bale of twenty-five pounds in weight, pressed into a solid mass and covered with hide and tarred cloth. It had, however, been six months on the way, had suffered from the curiosity of the custom house, and had thus lost much of its virtue by evaporation of the volatile element. Having at that time no opportunity for exact experiment, I chewed up the majority of the bale without other effect than a lessening of appetite and some of physical endurance. Being quite incredulous of the tales of the seemingly miraculous effects of Coca, I addressed a letter of inquiry to Dr. Alexander Stewart, of Peru, and received from him the following reply:

DEAR DOCTOR: My experience with Coca extends over four years, during which period the native hospital of Arica, having a daily average of thirty-five patients, afforded me ample opportunities for observing its effects. The patients were chiefly Indians from the interior, they being the principal users of the plant. They chew the leaves and, from their nutritive and power to allay hunger, they are enabled to travel day after day for three or four days without food or water. Thus they travel hundreds of miles through this arid country, water not being obtainable unless carried in calabashes. Statements set forth in Johnston's "Chemistry of Common Life," to which you refer, are true in almost every particular. The narcotic effect is not so prominent a feature as its power to prevent hunger, thirst, and need for sleep. I have frequently observed patients, when convalescing from fevers, using large quantities of it. It has also the power of mitigating the difficulty of breathing, haemoptysis, and drowsiness incident to traveling among the hills, 4000 meters above the sea. When going to Bolivia it was with difficulty the mule-driver could keep me awake. Only by repeated shaking could he accomplish that object, which was very necessary, as sleep under such circumstances is nearly always fatal. It is not an astringent. It does not in any way shorten life. With regard to this same point I have many communications from English gentlemen living in Bolivia for the past twenty years, and who have employed hundreds of these Cholos in their copper mines. They inform me that they have never seen any bad results from its use. On the contrary, natives have been found in the valleys overtaken by fever, and subsisting on it alone for several days. I never observed that it dilated the pupils. I believe that it would prove a valuable addition to the materia medica.

Yours truly,

ALEXANDER STEWART, M.R.e.S.

Dr. Stewart also kindly forwarded to me the following letter:

CORO CORO, PERU, May 29, 1866.

Dr. Stewart:

DEAR SIR: In answer to your inquiries regarding Coca, I would reply that I have resided in this place for six years. To each of our laborers we give one pound of Coca leaves weekly, and to the boys one half pound; they chew the leaves or drink the infusion. This takes away hunger and the need for sleep. A person may go forty-eight hours without food or sleep. Though totally unaccustomed to it, I have chewed one-quarter pound in one night, the only effect being to disperse all desire for sleep. Many workers consume two or three pounds weekly.

Yours truly, GEO. GASSETT

A Physician's Summary Of the Medical Benefits

It would not difficult to prolong the list of maladies in which Coca may prove and has proved valuable as a remedy, nor perhaps profitably to discuss its introduction into general use as a substitute for tea and coffee, and especially for chewing tobacco. I will indulge in one remark only.

That nervousness, many and to a degree before unknown in any country, is being rapidly developed in this land and age, is a melancholy fact to which the American physicians are being speedily opened. Our climate is stimulating, our habits are stimulating, the grounds for existence are stimulating, and human nature is over-driven on every side. May not Coca be destined to the grand palliative of these conditions, and the useful sustainer of exertion among our professional and business men? Contributing so marvelously to endurance both of mind and body, and doing this with certainly less injury to the system than any cognate substance known, I look to Coca as the great preserver of life and health in future generations.

From what has been said of the nature and effects of Coca it will be seen that I do not regard this plant the light of a drug, any more, at least, than coffee, tea, or tobacco can be so termed. Nor, indeed, is it as susceptible of application as a drug as those substances even; since its effects upon the body are by much disturbance than those of any of them. To be of value as a substance must have pathogenetic power. It is, then, not as a drug that we should regard though its sphere in medical practice is destined to be a very wide, and an immensely important one. Its place is that of a food, or, if you supplemental or adjunct to food. Its economic uses in the community will be of a high grade, and employment in the army, navy, merchant marine will be still higher. It will sustain the life of many an exhausted soldier and shipwrecked sailor. Had our army at Gettysburg been supplied with it, Lee and his troops would never have been allowed to re-cross the Potomac. A bale of it should form part of the supply of every ship, since, in case of shipwreck, it would sustain life much longer than a corresponding amount of food. Physiology teaches us that where there is use in the body, there is waste: where there is waste, there must be repair: for repair there must be food; and for food to become fitted repair, there must be digestion and assimilation. All this is true, but we must farther, and recall the fact that each mouthful contains a definite, fixed, and practically invariable amount of each element contained in the food. Doubtless the normal proportion of these elements would be the proper one to furnish suitable material for repair in case we were born ·physiologically perfect, and then lived physiologically.' But few of us are born with approach to perfection of structure, and none us can live physiologically.

And this for two reasons:
First: We do not know all of nature's laws.
And, second, we could not obey them if we did.

The demands of life, civilized or savage, prevent it. Probably nature demands that we should go naked. We cannot do it. It demands a proper relation of exercise, food, and sleep. We cannot attain to it; and so on *ad infinitum.* Now, consider the case of the sedentary man. Does he not waste his brain out of all proportion to his muscles? And is it not clear that to nourish brain, he must eat more muscle-food than he requires? And that at the best must not his brain often go hungry? What becomes of this overplus of muscle-food? Well, two things happen. If the man's stomach is feeble it refuses to digest so much food, and he develops dyspepsia. If he does digest it, and it is absorbed, his blood is filled up with material which he cannot or does not use: his liver becomes congested and, in ordinary parlance, he is bilious. Now, are not dyspepsia and biliousness *the* diseases, *par excellence,* of sedentary men? And is it not true that literary men, of inactive bodily habit and abstemious as to stimulants, are eaters? If you do not know you have only to ask any housewife who is accustomed to entertain the clergy-a class who avoid wine and tobacco, a part of whom only are able to take tea and coffee in sufficient amount to diminish excessive waste without rendering them nervous; and who are therefore obliged to eat hugely

For these and all classes in the community upon whom the demands of life are similar, Coca is, in my opinion, infinitely better than wine or tobacco, even with the addition of coffee and tea, and this for reasons already given. Only less important to the laboring classes is it, as bulk of the muscles and other of the body exceeds that of the brain. A surplus of brain food is of small account to the laborer compared with the surplus of food to the sedentary.

Fat can be stored up in the body or burnt as fuel, and phosphorus, etc., can be easily eliminated by the kidneys. The surplus, being much smaller this instance, can more easily disposed of. Still, he would be a bold man who would say that the laborer is liable to no disease through the lack of a proper relation of food to his exact wants. Now, it can be shown that tea, coffee, wine, tobacco, and, more than all, Coca, prevent waste. And not this alone, but they prevent excess of waste in parts excessively used, or called upon for an undue proportion of work. This way they help to balance up between the needs of the system, under strain of life, the constant and uniform proportion of the elements of food. Who shall measure the benefit of this effect? It is beyond all human computation.

If, then, my philosophy and physiology be correct, and if Coca is and does what is claimed, and what I believe it will proven to be and do, the introduction of this substance into general use is a matter of exceeding importance, and its employment should be fostered by every true physician.

Erythroxylon Coca - Its Botanical Character.

Coca is indigenous to South America. The different botanists disagree as to which exact family it should be assigned. Linnus, De Candolle, Payer, Raymundi of Lima, Huntk, and others, place it in the family of the Erythroxyleae, of which there exists but one genus, the Erythroxylon, while Jussien adopts another classification and places it in the family of the Malpighiaceae (genus Sethia). Lamarck, on the contrary, believes that this plant should be classed among the family of Nerprem (Rhamnae).

Erythroxylon Coca is a shrub which reaches a height of from six to nine feet and the stem is of about the thickness of a finger. In our climate it cannot thrive except in a hot-house, and there its height does not exceed one metre.

The root, rather thick, shows multiple and uniform divisions; its trunk is covered with a ridged bark, rugged, nearly always glabrous, and of a whitish color. Its boughs and branches, rather numerous, are alternant, sometimes covered with thorns when the plant is cultivated in a soil which is not well adapted to it.

The leaves, which fall spontaneously at the end of each season, are alternate, petiolate, with double intra-accillary stipules at the base. In shape they are elliptical-lanceolate, their size varying according to the nature of the plant or of the soil in which it grows.

The leaf of Coca gathered in Peru, of which we give two figures of the natural size, is generally larger and thicker than the leaf of the Bolivian Coca. It is also richer in the alkaloid, consequently much more bitter.

The Coca leaf from Bolivia, smaller than the Peruvian leaf, is as much esteemed as the latter, although it contains less of the alkaloid. It possesses so exquisite and so soft an aroma, indeed, that the coqueros seek it in preference to any other.

The Coca leaves of Brazil and Colombia are much smaller than those of Peru and Bolivia. Their color is much paler. Containing but traces of the alkaloid they are not bitter, and possess a pleasant, but very volatile aroma.

One of the most important characteristics of the Coca leaf is the disposition of its nervures; parallel with the midrib two longitudinal projections are to be seen, which, starting from the base of the leaf, extend in a gentle curve to its point.

The upper surface of these leaves is of a beautiful green tint; the lower surface of a paler green, except, however, near the midrib. At this point, there is a strip of green darker than the rest, which becomes brown in the withered leaves.

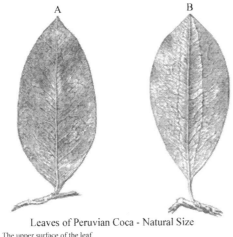

Leaves of Peruvian Coca - Natural Size
A. The upper surface of the leaf
B. Lower surface showing the projecting veins on either side of the mid-rib

The flowers, small, regular and hermaphrodite, white or greenish yellow, are found either alone or in groups in little bunches of cyme at the axil of the leaves or bracts, which take their place on certain branches. The disposition into cymes is that most commonly met with. They are supported by a slender pedicel, somewhat inflated at the top, the length of which does not exceed one centimetre. The sepals, joined at the base and lanceolated, are of a green tint with a whitish top. The petals, half a centimetre in length, pointed, concave inside and yellowish white, exhale a rather pleasant odor. They are provided with an exterior appendage, of the same color and of the same consistency, surmounted on each side with an ascending fimbriated leaf, irregularly triangular in shape. The stamens, at first joined in a tube for one-third of their length, afterward separate into white subulated strings, provided with an obtuse ovoid anther which extends a little beyond the petals. The ovary is ovoid in shape and green in color, thickening at the top into a yellowish glandular tissue. The style which rises above it separates into three diverging branches, provided with orbicular papilliform bodies at their extremity, obliquely inserted into the slender patina. The fruit is a drupe of an elongated ovoid form, being a little more than a centimetre in length, of a reddish color when fresh, and having a tender, thickish pulp inclosing a seed. This seed shows longitudinal furrows and alternate vertical projections which make its division irregularly hexagonal. When the fruit is dried, the skin assumes a brownish color, shrivels up and molds itself on the protuberances and irregularities of the seed.

Some Regional Variations of Coca

Some botanists have considered the characteristic lateral lines of the Coca leaf as nerves. Martins was of the opinion these result from pressure of the margin of the leaf as it is rolled toward the midrib while in the bud, the pinching of the tissue causing the substance of the leaf to be raised, resembling a delicate nerve. The lines have been designated as "tissue folds,"** but there is no fold in either the epidermis or substance of the leaf. Histologically the lines are formed by a narrow band of elongated cells, which resemble the collenchyma cells of the neighboring epidermis, and these doubtless serve to stiffen the blade. The lines have no connection with the veins of the leaf and in transmitted light seem like mere ghostly shadows which vanish under closer search.

Many observers have supposed they had found the original locality of wild Coca. Alcide d'Orbigny describes in his travels, having entered a valley covered with what he supposed to be the wild Coca shrub, but thinking he might be mistaken, he showed the plant to his mule driver, who was the proprietor of a cocal in Yungas, and he pronounced it undoubtedly Coca and gathered a quantity of the leaves. It has been asserted that wild Coca may be found in the province of Cochero, and one of the former governors of Oran, in the province of Salta, on the northern borders of the Argentine Republic, claims to have found wild Coca of excellent quality in the forests of that district. Poeppig also described having found wild specimens, known by the natives as Mama Coca, in the Cerro San Cristobal, near the Huallaga, some miles below Huanueo. These examples closely resemble the shrubs of cultivated Coca collected by Martins in the neighborhood of Ega, Brazil, near the borders of the Amazon, and correspond to the wild specimens commonly found throughout Peru.

In Colombia Humboldt, Bonpland and Kunth described Erythroxylon Hondense as the possible type of the originally cultivated Coca shrub, but there is a difference between the leaves of E. Coca and E. Hondense in the arrangement of their nervures, from which Pyrame de Candolle considers them as entirely distinct species. Andre speaks of Coca in the valley of the river Cauca as in abundance in both the wild and half-wild state, but an excellent authority denies that Coca is found wild in Colombia. The exact locality where Coca is indigenous in a wild state has, however, never been determined. Though there are many Coca plants growing throughout the montana outside of cultivation, it is presumed that these are examples where the seeds of the plant have either been unintentionally scattered or else are the remains of some neglected plantation where might have flourished a vigorous cocal under the Spanish reign. There are evidences of these scattered shrubs throughout the entire region where Coca will grow, but there is no historical data to base a conclusion that these represent wild plants of any distinct original variety, while the weight of testimony indicates that they are examples of the traditional plant which have escaped from cultivation.

Although the heart of the habitat of Coca is in the Peruvian montana from 7° S., north for some ten degrees, the shrubs are found scattered along the entire eastern curve of the Andes, from the Straits of Magellan to the borders of the Caribbean Sea, in the moist and warm slopes of the mountains, at an elevation from 1,500 to 5,000 and even 6,000 feet, being cultivated at a higher altitude through Bolivia than in Peru. Throughout this extent there are to be seen large plantations and many smaller patches where Coca is raised in a small way by Indians who come three or four times a year to look after their crop. In some localities, through many miles, these cocals cover the sides of the mountains for thousands of feet. During the Incan period the centre of this industry was about the royal city of Cuzco, and at present the provinces of Caravaya and of Sandia, east of Cuzco, are the sites of the finest variety of Peruvian grown Coca. In this same region there grows coffee, cacao, cascarilla, potatoes, maize, the sugar cane, bananas, peaches, oranges, paltas, and a host of luscious fruits and many valuable dyes and woods.

There are still important Coca regions about Cuzco, and at Paucartambo and in several Indian towns along the Ilnanuco valley, situated in the very heart of the northern Montana and noted for its coffee plantations. At one time this region was accredited with supplying Coca for all Peru, which probably meant the mining centres of Huancavelica—formerly more prominent than at present—and Cerro de Pasco, where the mines are still extensively worked. There are fine cocals at Mayro, on the Zuzu Piver, and at Pozuso—which are German colonies; at the latter place is located the laboratory of Kitz, one of the largest manufacturers of crude cocaine, whose product supplies some of the important German chemical houses. Still further to the northwest—in Colombia, there are a number of small plantations along the valley of Yupa, at the foot of the chain of mountains which separates the province of Santa Marta de Maracaibo, at the mouth of the Magdalena River. Eastward from the Montana Coca is cultivated near many of the tributaries of the Amazon, and through some portions of Brazil, where it is known as ypadu. The Amazonian plant is not only modified in appearance, but the alkaloidal yield is inferior.

Commentaries on the Cultivation of Coca

Erythroxylon Coca appears to have come originally from Peru, and from there its cultivation was carried into Bolivia, Ecuador, New Grenada, and Brazil, in a word, throughout the entire torrid zone of South America.

For some time, as a result of the extended consumption of Coca and for a still stronger reason, now that the day is at hand when the consumption of Coca will assume greater proportions, numerous plantations of Coca trees have been laid out in regions where that shrub was formerly unknown. We take pleasure in recording that these attempts have proved successful in the Antilles, thanks to the disinterested sacrifices of our friend, Dr. Bétancès. It is also with pleasure that we present anew an interesting communication made by the learned doctor to the "Société d'Acclimatation de France" as appeared in the Revue Diplomatique, 17th of March, 1888.

"Dr. Bétancès has succeeded in acclimatizing Coca in the Antilles. At considerable expense and after numerous shipments of seeds and the transportation of plants (this with the greatest difficulty) to Porto Rico and San Domingo, Dr. Bétancès had the pleasure of receiving a fine branch of Coca in full bloom, which was sent to him by Monseigneur Merello, Archbishop of San Domingo. This twig, which the members of the Society were enabled to examine, excited the most lively curiosity and won the commendation of M. Geoffroy Saint-Hilaire. It was raised from a plant which had been only eighteen months under cultivation."

"In Porto Rico the plant reaches a greater height than in Peru.

"A box filled with beautiful leaves has also been received by Dr. Bétancès and forwarded to Mr. Mariani. This also came from Monseigneur Mereflo.

It is therefore evident that the plant can be cultivated in the Antilles and that it may become a source of wealth to that country."

Plantations like this would probably thrive in Corsica or Algeria, countries where the temperature at certain points is somewhat analogous to that of the tropics.

It is a fact that this shrub does not attain its complete development except in countries where the mean temperature is from fifteen to eighteen degrees centigrade.

But heat does not suffice; great humidity is also necessary to Coca Therefore it is met with principally on the sides of hills and at the bottom of wooded valleys which abound on both sides of the Cordillieras. Unfortunately, these regions are rather distant from the coast and they are, furthermore, devoid of easy means of communication; it is above all to this particular cause, the difficulty of transportation, that we must attribute the relatively high price of Coca leaves.

The cultivation of Coca trees is begun by sowing the seed in beds called Almazigos. As soon as the plant appears it is protected from the heat of the sun by means of screens and matting; when it reaches a height of from 40 to 50 centimetres, it is transferred to furrows 18 centimetres in length by 7 in depth, care being taken that each plant is separated from its neighbor by a distance of a foot.

During the first year maize is sown in the interspaces, rapidly overreaching the shrub, and taking the place of the screens and mats.

The growth of the shrub is rather rapid, reaching its full height in about five years. But the time when it becomes productive precedes that at which it attains its complete height by about 3 years after being planted.

After that, when the season has been especially damp, it yields as often as four times a year. Attempts have been made to acclimatize it in Europe, but so far without success. As early as 1869 the cultivation of it was tried in the Botanical Garden of Hyères, but no satisfactory result was obtained. We presented, in 1872, two samples to the appreciative and learned director of the Garden of Acclimatization of Paris, M. Geoffroy Saint-Hilaire, and notwithstanding all the care taken of the young plants, they failed to reach their full growth. Several frail Coca plants may be seen in the conservatories of the Jardin des Plantes de Paris, in the Botanical Gardens of London, of Brussels etc., likewise at several great horticulturists of Gand, notably Van Houten's.

The Gathering & Drying Of Coca

The plant begins to yield when it is about a year and a half old. The leaf is the only part of the plant used. It should be gathered in dry weather; this is entrusted generally to women, and simply consists in plucking each leaf with the fingers.

The leaves are received into aprons, carefully carried under sheds, to shelter them from the rain and dampness, dried, and then packed.

We quote from the Voyage dans la region du Titicaca, by Paul Marcoy, the following passage (" Tour of the World," May, 1877): "Of all the valleys of the Carabaya group, Ituata is the one where Coca is cultivated on the largest scale. They were then at the height of the work, peons and peonnes were following each other through the plantations of the shrub, so dear to the natives that a decree of 1825 placed it in the crown of the arms of Peru, alongside of the vicunia and cornucopia, or horn-of-plenty. Men and women carried a cloth slung across the shoulders in which were placed the leaves, as they gathered them one by one. These leaves, spread out on large awnings, were exposed to the sun for two or three days, then packed up in bags of about one metre in size and sent off to all parts of the territory.

This gathering of the Coca is just such an occasion for rejoicing for the natives of the valleys, as reaping-time and harvests are for our peasants. On the day when the gathering of the leaves is finished both sexes that have taken part in the work assemble and celebrate, in dances and libations, the pleasure they experience in having finished their labors."

In 1851, the annual production of Bolivia was estimated to be more than 400,000 certos (600,000 kilogrammes) of Coca leaves, of which three-quarters came from the province of Yungas.

Traditional Indian Coca Cultivation

Environmental Conditions

The temperature in which Coca is grown must be equable, of about 18° C. (61.4° F.). If the mean exceeds 20° C. (68° F.), the plant loses strength and the leaf assumes a dryness which always indicates that it is grown in too warm a situation, and though the leaves may be more prolific, they have not the delicate aroma of choice Coca. It is for the purpose of securing uniform temperature and appropriate drainage that Coca by preference is grown at an altitude above the intense heat of the valleys, and where it is virtually one season throughout the year, the only change being between the hot sun and the profuse rains of the tropical Montana. As the temperature lowers with increase of altitude, when too great a height is reached the shrub is less thrifty and develops a small leaf of little market value, while as only one harvest is possible the expense of cultivation is too great to prove profitable.

Even close to the equator, in the higher elevations, there is always danger from frost, and for this reason some of the cocals about Huanuco have at times suffered serious loss. All attempts at Coca cultivation on a profitable scale near to Lima have failed not only because of the absence of rain, but because of the sometimes extended cold season.

Types of Earth Most Suitable

A peculiar earth is required for the most favorable cultivation of Coca, one rich in mineral matter, yet free from limestone, which is so detrimental that even when it is in the substratum of a vegetable soil the shrub grown over it will be stunted and the foliage scanty. While the young Coca plants may thrive best in a light, porous soil, such as that in the warmer valleys, the full grown shrub yields a better quality of leaf when grown in clay. The red clay, common in the tropical Andes, is formed by a union of organic acids with the inorganic bases of alkaline earths, and oxides—chiefly of iron which in a soluble form are brought to the surface by capillarity.

These elements enter the Coca shrub in solution through its multiple fibrous roots, which look like a veritable wig. The delicate filaments are extended in every direction to drink in moisture, and as these root-hairs enter the interspaces of the soil, the particles of which are covered with a film of water, absorption readily takes place. The clay soil of the Montana affords this property in a high degree, while the hillside cultivation admits of an appropriate drainage the interspaces without which the delicate root would soon be rotted. As the water is absorbed from the soil, a flow by capillarity lakes place to that point, and so the Coca root will drain a considerable space.

It is possible a metallic soil may have some marked influence on the yield of alkaloid. At Phara, where the best Coca leaves are grown, the adjacent mountains are formed of at least two per cent, of arsenical pyrites, a fact which is noteworthy because this is the only place in Peru where the soil is of such a nature. Most of the soil of the Andean hills where the best Coca is grown, originates in the decay of the pyritiferous schists, which form the chief geological feature of the surrounding mountains. This, commonly mixed with organic matter and salts from the decaying vegetation, or that of the trees burned to make a clearing, affords what might be termed a virgin earth - terre franche ou normale - which requires no addition of manures for invigoration. In the conservatory it has been found, after careful experimentation, that a mixture of leaf mould and sand - terre de bruyere - forms the best artificial soil for the Coca plant.

The Importance of Humidity

Aside from an appropriate soil that is well drained, there is another important element to the best growth of Coca, and that is a humid atmosphere. Indeed, in the heart of the Montana it is either hazy or drizzling during some portion of the day throughout the year, the intense glare of the tropical sun being usually masked by banks of fog, so that it would seem that one living here is dwelling in the clouds. At night the atmosphere is loaded with moisture and the temperature may be a little lower than during the day, though there is usually but a trifling variation day after day.

The natural life of the Coca shrub exceeds the average life of man, yet new Cocals are being frequently set out to replace those plants destroyed through accident or carelessness. The young plants are usually started in a nursery, or almaciga, from seeds planted during the rainy season, or these may be propagated from cuttings. In the conservatory slips may be successfully grown if care is taken to retain sufficient moisture about the young plant by covering it with a bell glass.

Protecting Seeds & Seedlings

The birds are great lovers of Coca seeds, and when these are lightly sown on the surface of the nursery it is necessary to cover the beds at night with cloths to guard against "picking and stealing." Before sowing the seeds are sometimes germinated by keeping them in a heap three or four inches high and watering them until they sprout. They are then carefully picked apart and planted either in hills or the seeds are simply sown on the surface of the ground, and from that they take them up and set them in other places into earth that is well labored and tilled and made convenient to set them in. There is commonly over the beds of the nursery a thatched roof - huasichi - which serves as a protection to the tender growing shoots from the beating rain or melting fierceness of the occasional sun. The first spears are seen in a fortnight, and the plants are carefully nourished during six months, or perhaps even a year until they become strong enough to be transplanted to the field.

Planting Out & Cultivating Coca

As a rule, all plants that are forty or fifty centimetres high (16 to 20 inches) may be set out, being placed in rows as we might plant peas or beans. In some cases they are set in little walled beds, termed aspi, a foot square, care being taken that the roots shall penetrate straight into the ground. Each of these holes is set about with stones to prevent the surrounding earth from falling, while yet admitting a free access of air about the roots. In such a bed three or four seedlings may be planted to grow up together, a method which is the outgrowth of laziness, as the shrubs will flourish better when set out singly. Usually the plants are arranged in rows, termed uachas, which are separated by little walls of earth - umachas - at the base of which the plants are set. In some districts the bottle gourd, maize, or even coffee, is sown between these rows, so as to afford a shield for the delicate shoots against sun or rain. At first the young plants are weeded - mazi as it is termed - frequently, and in an appropriate region there is no need for artificial watering: but the Coca plant loves moisture, and forty days under irrigation will cover naked shrubs with new leaves, but the quality is not equal to those grown by natural means.

The Processes of Harvesting

In from eighteen months to two years the first harvest, or mitta, which literally means time or season—is commenced. The leaves are considered mature when they have begun to assume a faint yellow tint, or better—when their softness is giving place to a tendency to crack or break off when bent, usually about eight days before the leaf would fall naturally. This ripe Coca leaf is termed by the Indians cacha.

The Coca shrub, growing out of immediate cultivation, will sometimes attain a height of about twelve feet, but for the convenience of picking, cultivated plants are kept down to less than half that height by pruning - huriar or ecuspar - at the time of harvesting, by picking off the upper twigs, which increases the lateral spread of the shrub. The first harvest—or rather preliminary picking, is known as quita calzon, from the Spanish quitar—to take away, and calzon—breeches. As the name indicates, it is really more of a trimming than what might be termed a harvest, and the leaves gathered at this time have less flavor than those of the regular mittas. Each of the harvests is designated by name—which may vary according to the district. The first regular one in the spring - mitta de marzo - yields the most abundantly. Then, at the end of June, there is commonly a scanty crop known as the mitta de San Juan - the harvest of the festival of St. John – while a third, following in October or November, is the mitta de Todos Santos—the harvest of all saints.

Usually the shrubs are weeded only after each harvest, and there seems to be a prejudice against doing this at other times, though if the cocals are kept clear the harvest may be anticipated by more than a fortnight. Garcilasso tells how an avaricious planter, by diligence in cultivating his Coca, got rid of two-thirds of his annual tithes in the first harvest.

Picking exerts a beneficial influence on the shrub, which otherwise would not flourish so well. The gathering – palla - is still done by women and children - palladores as they are termed - just as was the custom during the time of the Incas, though the Colombians will not permit women to take part in the Coca cultivation at any time.

Many writers have spoken of the extreme care with which the leaves are picked or pinched from the shrub, one by one; but to a casual observer the gathering seems to be done far more carelessly. The collector squats down in front of the shrub, and taking a branch strips the leaves off with both hands by a dexterous movement, while avoiding injury to the tender twigs. The pickers must be skilled in their work, for not only a certain knack, but some little force is requisite, as is shown by the wounds occasioned to even the hard skin of the hand of those who are accustomed to the task.

The leaves are collected in a poncho or in an apron of coarse wool, from which the green leaves - termed matu – are emptied into larger sacks - materos - in which they are conveyed to the drying shed - matucanclia. Four or five expert pickers in a good cocal can gather a cesta—equivalent to a bale of twenty-five pounds, in a day.

Harvesting is never commenced except when the weather is dry, for rain would immediately spoil the leaves after they have been picked, rendering them black in color and unsalable, a condition which the Indians term Coca gonupa, or yana Coca.

Coca when gathered is stored temporarily in sheds (matuhuarsi), which open into closed courts, the cachi, or matupampa, and the contents of these warehouses indicate the prosperity of the master of the cocal. In the drying yards of these places the leaves are spread in thin layers two or three inches deep, either upon a slate pavement – pizarra - or simply distributed upon a hard piece of clear ground of the casa de hacienda. The closest guardianship must now be maintained over the leaves during the process of drying, and on the slightest indication of rain they are swept under cover by the attendants with the greatest rapidity.

Drying may be completed within six hours in good weather, and when properly dried under such favorable conditions, the leaf is termed Coca del dia and commands the highest price. A well cured mature Coca leaf is olive green, pliable, clean, smooth and slightly glossy, while those which are old or are dried more slowly assume a brownish green and are less desirable. After drying, the leaves are thrown in a heap, where they remain about three days while undergoing a sort of sweating process. When this commences the leaf is crisp, but sweating renders it soft and pliable. After sweating the leaves are again sun dried for a half hour or so, and are then ready for packing. If the green leaves cannot be immediately dried, they may be preserved for a few days if care be taken not to keep them in heaps, which would induce a secondary sweating or decomposition and give rise to a musty odor, termed Coca cocaspada, which clings even to the preparations made from such leaves.

The refinement of curing maintains a certain amount of moisture in the leaf, together with the peculiar Coca aroma, and it is exact discernment in this process which preserves the delicacy of flavor. When drying has been so prolonged as to render the leaf brittle and without aroma, the quality of Coca is destroyed. It has been suggested that an improvement might be made in drying through the use of sheds, where the leaves could be exposed in layers to an artificial heat, and a current of dry air, after the manner of the secaderos used in Cuba for drying coffee. But whether because of an unwillingness to adopt new methods, or because of some peculiar influence of the atmosphere imparted to the leaf in the native way of drying, all attempts to employ artificial methods have proved unsatisfactory.

Selecting Coca Seeds for Planting

When the fruit has formed it changes color in ripening, through all the hues from a delicate greenish yellow to a deep scarlet vermilion, and upon the same shrub there may be a number of such colorations to be seen at one time. Monardes, writing centuries ago, said: "The fruit is in the form of a grape, and as the fruit of the myrtle is reddish when it is ripening, and about of the same dimensions- when attaining its highest maturity becoming darker black." I was going to say that the fruit resembles the smallest of oval cranberries, both in color and in shape, for I at one time found some little cranberries which appeared so much like the Coca fruit as to seem almost identical; but all cranberries are not alike, and there has already been too much confusion in hasty comparison, so I shall reserve my description for the more technical details. The fruit is gathered while yet scarlet during the March harvest, but if it is permitted to remain on the bush it becomes dark brown or black and shrivels to the irregular lobing of the contained nut.

In selecting the seeds care is taken to cast aside all fruit that is decayed, the balance being thrown into water, and those which are light enough to float are rejected as indicating they have been attacked by insects. The balance is then rotted in a damp, shaded place, to extract the seed, which is washed and sun dried. When it is desired to preserve these any length of time the fruit is exposed to the hot sun, which dries the fleshy portion into a protective coating. But the seeds do not keep well. In Peru perhaps they will retain germinating power for about fifteen days, while those from plants grown in the conservatory must be planted fresh, when still red, for if allowed to dry they become useless.

Pests & Predators of the Coca Plant

With every detail to cultivation which tradition has inspired, the Coca crop is not always secure, for the cocals are subject to the attacks of several pests, which, while a constant source of annoyance may at times seriously damage the shrubs. Below an altitude of four thousand feet there is the iilo, a little butterfly, which during a dry spell deposits its eggs, and as the grubs develop they devour the younger leaves. In the older cocals an insect called mougna sometimes introduces itself into the trunk of the shrub and occasions its withering.

M. Grandidier speaks of a disease termed cupa, or cuchupa, in the valley of the Santa Marta, which has destroyed an entire crop within eight days. From an attack of this not only the immediate leaf is rendered small and bitter, but during the following year the shrub remains unproductive, and a gall-like excrescence is developed termed saran mocllo—seeds of gall. Some cultivators at the first indication of this disease prune the affected twigs and so succeed in raising a new crop by the next harvest.

The ant, cuqui, which is a great pest through all the Montana, is a dangerous evil to the Coca plant. It not only cuts the roots, but disintegrates the bark and destroys the leaves, and in a single night may ruin an entire plantation. In fact, the sagacity of the traditional ant is outdone by these pests. Some of them are capable of carrying a kernel of corn, and an army of them will run off with a bag of corn in a night, kernel by kernel, making a distinct trail in the line of their depredations. They build their nests of leaves, twigs and earth, and even construct an underground system of channels to supply their hillocks with water. It is extremely difficult to keep them out of a cocal, as they will burrow under the deepest ditches, and the only method of being free from them is to destroy their hills wherever they are found.

Another enemy to the shrub is a long bluish earthworm, which eats the roots and so occasions the death of the plant. Then a peculiar fungus, known as taja, forms at times on the tender twigs, occasioned by injury or from poor nutrition. Aside from these pests, there are a number of weeds which are particularly injurious to Coca, among which are the Panicuni platicaule, P. scandens, P. decumheus, Pannisetum Perurianum, Drimaria, and Pteris arachnoidea.'" These plants grow rapidly and take so much nourishment from the soil as to destroy the nutrition of the Coca shrub. For a similar reason the planting of anything between the rows is now abandoned.

Summary of Coca Cultivation Techniques

The plant grows well at altitudes ranging from 1000 to 6000' above sea level. In Peru cocaine is grown between 700 and 2300 metres; in Ceylon, at right around 650 metres; and in the East Indies from 350 to 800 metres. The ideal average temperature for vigor in growth is 68°F. Coca will not tolerate freezing temperatures in the night or temperatures above 95° for extended periods in the day. At the higher part of the temperature range the plant loses much of its vital force, the leaves become dry and the subtle tang of the essential oils is lost. At the lower end of the range the plant becomes dispirited, the leaves remain small, never fully maturing, and the plant cannot be counted on to give more than one lackluster harvest a year.

While the plant thrives in locations where it receives lots of direct sunlight, it will also do well enough if it must be grown in a relatively shady spot, though it will not show as lush a leaf population at maturity. There is relatively little difference in alkaloid production between shade-grown and sun-grown Coca, though the sparse harvests from the shaded tree do mean significantly less production overall. Coca cannot be effectively cultivated in regions which experience long dry spells, and does best when there is a certain temperate humidity in the air for most or all of the year. It is most desirable that there be a constant, or as near constant as possible humidity throughout the year, a situation which bodes well for greenhouse cultivation. Neither should the rainy season experienced by the plant be extended, for while a great deal of rain makes for a big, gloriously bushed plant, it somehow diminishes the alkaloid production of the profuse leaves, thus stranding the cultivator with a fine harvest of glossy leaves and the prospect of very sore jaw muscles if he is to obtain any of the benefits hoped for in his long efforts.

Several writers on the subject of Coca cultivation have noted that any area suitable for the growing of Tea plants is also eminently suited for Coca cultivation, a fact that might make consultation with your friendly agricultural department a bit less trying if you need assistance in locating a suitable area for any project you might have in mind.

One starts Coca by planting the seeds in covered beds which protect the sprouts from the direct sun and from battering rains, not to mention the predations of various creatures. The seeds are planted three inches apart. Those selected for planting should be well-ripened, and should be air-dried in a breezy, shaded spot for three days before going into the earth. It is not absolutely necessary to engage in the perhaps perilous business of transplantation; in several places seeds are planted directly into the furrows. In such cases the furrows are covered with a layer of non-acid leaves or with bedding plastic.

Bedded seeds as well as field-planted seeds should be planted 3/4 inches deep, and should not be watered for several days, and then only sparingly. Culture of Coca requires no special soil other than an adequate supply of humus and sufficient sand/clay to stabilize the soil without loss of permeability.

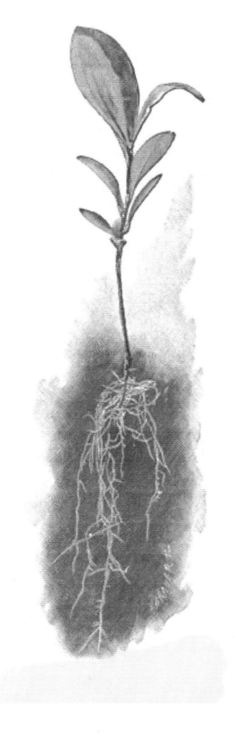

After from two to three weeks the seeds germinate, and one then begins a gradual buildup of exposure of the sprouts to sunlight, at the rate of one hour the first day, two hours the second, and so forth until the sprouts are accustomed to the full daylight cycle in which they will be living. If one does not go through this acclimatization process the little plants will elongate severely and many will topple of their own abnormally stimulated weight, defeated by their Icarus-like reach for the living sun.

During the first six months of their life the little Coca plants are very susceptible to rots and moulds, and any part or plant thus afflicted should be removed immediately. Also one should dust the plants for insect pests regularly during the first six months.

In around 2 1/2 months the plants will reach a height of 5". This will be the time to transplant if you have bedded them. One takes a wide, deep ball up with each plant and sets them out on rows, two feet apart, with the rows themselves spaced at three foot intervals. Other spacing arrangements mentioned in the literature on Coca planting include plots of 2.5'x 2.5'; 3' x 3'; or, upon occasion, notably in hill country, of 2' x 6'.

After 18 months it is possible to make the premier, most gentle of harvests. The young trees at this point are very tender and can be badly or fatally wounded by a ham-handed harvest. Your first harvest will not be abundant; however its passage will mark the beginning of a period when you will be able to obtain several good harvests a year, so practice restraint. A light harvest stimulates the plant at this and all other points, but with the first effort one should take no more than 25% of the leaves, and should leave most of the lower leaves alone. The first harvest must be performed during the dryer part of the year or, in greenhouse cultivation, after a period when the humidity in the air has been gradually drawn down over a period of months. With this first harvest, the plant is pruned back to a height of one foot above the ground and the lateral branches near the bottom are lightly trimmed back to assist the plant in attaining a solid profile conducive to maximum leaf production later on. The cultivator may expect the equivalent of from four to seven mature leaves from the average plant at first harvest.

Leaf production and alkaloid strength peak during the 5th-8th years of life, falling off gradually as the plant enters middle age. The Coca of Peru is expected to live for forty years, and this figure seems to hold around the world, though in some places - Java, in particular - the Coca plantations were razed and re-planted every eight years.

In the fourth or fifth year, when the plants have reached a height of from 3.5 to 4.5 feet, the planters of Peru and Java practiced their first grand harvest, though they harvested carefully and intermittently before that time beginning, as mentioned, at about 11/2 years. Upon occasion one finds planters who make the grand harvest their first, foregoing all previous possible opportunities. This seems to be a matter of personal choice and feeling for the state of health of the plant rather than a practice with specific biological basis. In the grand harvest, workers with very sharp, thin-bladed shears pass down the rows of plants cutting each back to a height of 2.5' and trimming back the lower laterals significantly, though not rendering them barren. The yield from such a first harvest on a typical 80 x 80 metre plantation was calculated to be 240 kilos of leaves.

After the first grand harvest the trees were left to bud and put forth new branches; as soon as these new shoots were well-established, in about six to eight weeks, they were trimmed back once again, before leaf development could begin. With the execution of this second trauma the trees were left alone for six months, and the results were that by the end of their rest period every tree had numerous small, hardy and luxuriant branches, bursting with new leaf.

Beginning, in a sense, with this point in the life of the plant, Coca production can be carried out in earnest. Depending upon the planter harvesting can take place from twice monthly to once every two or three months from this point on. The shorter the period between harvests, however, the more attentive the planter must be to rotating his picking around the needs of his trees - he must pick only a portion of the younger age-groups of leaves. A planter must harvest at least once every three months to prevent his trees from going into seed, thus diverting their vegetative energies from leaf production to seed nurture.

When an 80 x 80 metre plantation is harvested according to any of the above suggested schedules, the planters expect an annual yield of from 800 to 950 kilos, and the amount doesn't seem to vary much depending on the intervals chosen.

Coca and its therapeutic application
Angelo Mariani

The World of Vin Mariani

Arguably the greatest of the Coca entrepreneurs of the 19th century was Angelo Mariani, inventor of the cure-all tonic Vin Mariani. This energetic French/Italian medical entrepreneur was involved in every stage of coca production from seed to final product, and his Vin Mariani held a special place in the pharmacy of thousands of 19th century doctors. The following excepts from his prolific 19th century writings will give you some flavor of the wide-ranging intellect of this rogue pharmaceutical entrepreneur.

Of Coca and Its True Therapeutic Properties.

On chewing Coca leaves one feels a certain dryness of the throat, it produces at the same time a hypersecretion of the salivary glands, and a short while afterward the mucous membrane of the mouth is to a certain extent anesthetized. On its arrival in the stomach, the secretion of the gastric is increased, also the beating of the pulse; the rises about one-half and the urinary secretion is far from diminished.

Dr. Rabuteau found this in patients afflicted with gout, rheumatism and he has also found under the active influence of Coca, an increase of urea of about 10 per cent took place. Dr. Chas. Fauvel is another one of the first physicians who has experimented clinically with this plant. In a remarkable work, which he published some time ago, Dr. Fauvel praises Coca very highly in affections of the pharynx and of the larynx, and mentions in support of his recommendations several observations of granulous pharyngitis which had resisted all kinds of treatment, but which be had completely cured by the use of *Vin Mariani*.

Among all the pharmaceutical of which Coca is the base, we must mention especially the wine prepared by M. Mariani. This skillful chemist has succeeded in so dissolving the active principles of Coca, in a wine that contains already some tannin and traces of iron, that he has made of the whole a tonic *"par excellence."* This wine is not only agreeable to the taste, but also has the virtue of never constipating; it is, therefore, a thousand times preferable to the different preparations of Cinchona Wine, of which the overrated has fallen considerably since has taken possession of it.

Here are Mariani's comments on the cultivation of Coca.

Proper Cultivation Techniques

A light and sandy soil, a mean temperature of from fifteen to eighteen and a certain quantity of moisture, are the essential conditions for the perfect growth of Coca. According to Papig, in the valleys of Chincao and Oassapit, the ground where Coca best flourishes is slanting, relatively steep, but very fertile, composed of brick-red clay, containing probably some iron. Coca seeds are sown in beds, called "almazigos." The young plants are protected from the heat of the sun's rays by means of straw mats, or woven branches, and are afterward transplanted in furrows about 18 centimetres wide, and 8 deep, about 1 foot apart from each other. Under the beneficial influence of the sun and rain, the growth of the young tree is rapid; it blossoms at the end of from four .to six months, and soon yields seed. The Coca tree attains its complete height (two metres and a half on an average) at the end of about five years.

Attempts have been made to acclimatize it in Europe, but so far without success. Frail specimens may be found in the botanical gardens of and other cities, and also at the establishments of some of the great horticulturists of Belgium. We have given some samples of the plant to the esteemed director of the *Jardin Zoologique d'acclimatation* of Paris, Mr. Geoffroy Saint-Hilaire, who had them placed in the conservatories of the where the public are admitted to see them. Corsica and Algiers seem to possess the climatic conditions necessary for the perfect development of the Coca, and for that reason it is in these two countries where we shall pursue our efforts of culture.

Harvesting For Maximum Purity & Potency

The plant commences to give its first crop at the end of about one year and a half. The gathering must be done in dry weather; it is generally confined to women, and consists simply in detaching each leaf with the fingers. The leaves are collected in aprons, stored with care under awnings or in bags, sheltered from rain and dampness, dried, and then packed.

We quote from "Voyage in the Region of the Titicaca," published in "Around the World," May, 1877: Of all the valleys of the group of Carabaya, Ituata is the one where the Coca is cultivated on the largest scale. were then in full harvest; peons and peonnes followed each other through the plantations of that shrub, so

dear to the natives that a decree of 1825 had it placed in the coat of arms of Peru, together with the vicuna, and the cornucopia or horn of plenty. Men and women carried, slung over their shoulders, cloths in which were placed the leaves they had gathered one by one. These leaves, spread out on large mattings, were exposed to the sun's rays for two or three days, and then packed up in bags of about one metre in size, and sent over the entire territory. This harvesting of Coca is for the natives of the valleys an occasion of great rejoicing, as is for our farmers their harvest and vintage time. Oh the day when all the crop is gathered in, both sexes meet, and celebrate it by dancing, drinking, and various sports."

Preparation of the Harvest

If the cultivator has only a few trees for personal use, chances are that he will not be engaged in production of any finished product but, rather, will simply follow the time-honored consumption ritual of the coquero, who, whenever the spirit moves him, plucks a fresh leaf or two and chews. On the Coca plantations, however, the Coca is intended for further processing and is treated in the following manner.

The fresh leaves are spread evenly and thinly on flat metal trays. Clumps of leaves are broken up, and care is taken to assure that each leaf has maximum exposure to the air. With this precaution, fermentation and mould-formation can be avoided. Either of these problems causes great trouble as odor, color and strength will be adversely affected. The leaves are laid out on their drying pans in warm, windy shade on a hot, dry day. They are never exposed to the direct sun in drying. If they are being dried artificially the heat must be blown across them at a point no greater than 120°F., with plenty of fresh-air ventilation. There are a number of studies showing a drop in effective alkaloid content of from .34% by weight in the fresh state to .14% by weight after exposure to the direct sun for only three hours.

Whatever the process used, the leaf is considered dry when it can be broken cleanly by bending slightly, and the average time for drying in a hot, dry environment is from 36 to 40 hours. Needless to say, the leaves must be protected from nighttime moisture.

The dried leaves are taken and pulverized - the devices used vary from area to area. The powder obtained should be uniform, and should be immediately placed in airtight containers. This powder then forms the basis for further processing into refined Cocaine. The techniques by which the raw powder is converted to crystalline Cocaine are several, and are not complicated; however, there are several books on the subject available and since my interests lie in the botany and cultivation of drug plants and not in the chemical processes which render it into synthesized forms, I'll simply suggest that the interested reader refer to History of Coca (And/Or Press) or Psychedelic Chemistry by Michael Valentine Smith (Rip Off Press).

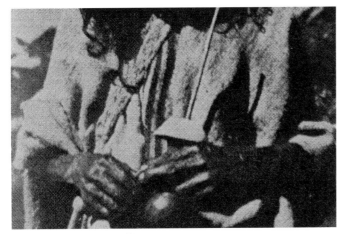

SECTION THREE: CULTIVATION & USE OF THE OPIUM POPPY

Some Preliminary Cautions Regarding Home-Growing

This book is intended to give information to those who need it for self-treatment of a disease or condition where one or more of the three great traditional medicinal plants, opium, coca and cannabis have proven effective. **Please become very familiar with the laws in your community which may prohibit growing one or more of these plants and which may impose severe penalties for doing so.**

That said, you may still want to try your hand at growing a crop of poppies just because they are a beautiful flower and the seeds do have culinary applications. There are plenty of places that sell seeds online – just google the exact phrase 'papaver somniferum seeds' and you'll get lots of results.

The key when ordering these seeds is to be discreet. Questions like "which variety will give me the strongest opium?" are strictly taboo. Your interest should lie in the color, height, hardiness for your zone etc. In other words, you are ordering a flowering plant for your garden. As long as you haven't begun incising your pods lets hope that if necessary you can legitimately claim that the plants were just ornamentals and that you use their seeds for baking.

Up until the point where you begin incising the capsules you may have plausible deniability – "I didn't know those were illegal – I just thought they were pretty flowers!". However, once you start collecting the juice from the capsules it is too late to deny you know what you are doing. This means that you should really think though where you are going to plant your crop so that if you decide to incise a few capsules just as an experiment there won't be any unwanted consequences.

A Poem on the Cultivation of the Medicinal Poppy

"The ying-su is a good plant to have. It is called ying because, though small, it is shaped like a fine vase; it is called su because the little seeds look like those of millet. When first growing it may be eaten like the vegetables of spring. When ground, the seeds and head yield a sap like cow's milk; when boiled, this becomes a drink fit for Buddha. Old men whose powers have decayed, who have little appetite, who when they eat meat cannot digest it and when they eat vegetables cannot distinguish their flavor, should take this drink. Use a willow mallet and a stone basin to beat it. Boil it in water sweetened with honey. It does good to the mouth and the throat. It restores tranquility to the lungs and nourishes the stomach."

"For three years now the door has been closed. I have gone nowhere and come back from nowhere. I see here the hermit of the shade and the long-robed priest; when they sit opposite I forget to speak. Then I have but to drink a cup of Poppy nectar. I laugh. I am happy. I have come to Ying-ch'uan, and am wandering the banks of the river there. I am climbing the slopes of the Lu Mountain in the far west."
(Su Che, early Tang Dynasty)

The Opium Poppy – A Brief Overview

Papaver Somniferum, the Opium Poppy, is a drug plant with a vast array of forms and colors, and shows a very sensitive range of responses to environment and handling. It is a relatively easy plant to cultivate once one is aware of its needs, which are not complex. It is of course, an illegal plant, but its legal status does not seem to trouble somniferum terribly, since it may be found growing wild in many parts of the world including the United States and Europe. Most uncultivated poppy plants will respond very nicely to attention and will, after two or three generations, slip back into the fold of productive garden beauties capable of producing a high-alkaloid gum when incised at the proper season.

There are great numbers of poppy species which do not produce opium alkaloids, and somniferum is the only one which does, with the exception of Papaver setigerum, a wild thistle-like poppy which grows along the northern Mediterranean coast, so let's open our discussion of the Opium Poppy by differentiating it from all other poppies which the amateur botanist stalking through the fields of Europe and North America in search of this specific garden companion is likely to encounter.

Identification of the Opium Poppy

It is almost impossible to give a general description of the Opium Poppy which will satisfy criteria for botanical classification, but since that is probably not the purpose of the search, it is possible to give some practical advice on identifying the uncultivated plant.

Since one will probably be going after the wild or uncultivated plant, and therefore will be dealing with a plant which has adapted its growth cycle to the seasonal change of its environment, the time to begin searching in the temperate zones of the northern hemisphere will be around late May or early June. By this time the wild flower will have

completed its growth cycle and will be on the verge of dropping off its petals and commencing the formation of its characteristic capsule. It is by the capsule that one may most easily identify the Opium

Poppy, differentiating it from the many other poppies which flourish in the wild state but do not form capsules. Earlier, before the formation of the capsule, the Opium Poppy, particularly in the wild state where there may be a great deal of variation in size of the plant, color and configuration of the flower and so forth, may easily be confused with non-alkaloid producing poppy plants. So, it will generally be best to set out on a field trip in the very late spring or early summer in either North America or Europe.

Where to look? As a general rule, anywhere where in former times people might have cultivated ornamental plants. The Opium Poppy is not an energetically escaping plant, and wild descendants of once cultivated garden poppies tend to stay pretty much around the old home grounds. Since the Opium Poppy was for many years extensively cultivated as an ornamental plant, it makes sense to begin with a search of abandoned house sites, old farms, roadways where once some soul may lovingly have decorated the verge for the delight of passers-by - all such places. In addition, I have found it both productive and delightful to take long slow walks through older small towns, keeping my eye out for houses which appear to have been built before about 1920, which have run-down yards where once there was obviously a garden. I have seen Opium Poppies growing in such yards in many states, but particularly in the far west and the mid-west, with Oregon, Ohio and Illinois topping the list in this informal little survey. In Europe I have found the Opium Poppy growing unattended (apparently) in the Netherlands, Belgium and France, though one finds far fewer abandoned homesites and run-down yards in Europe than one encounters in the United States. And, of course, one may also find, as I have in several cases, Opium Poppies being cultivated with care and attention because of their lovely nature by people who perhaps were unaware of their more versatile properties. For some unfathomable reason this seems to occur quite often in Ohio particularly.

What to look for? As I mentioned earlier, there is tremendous variation in the size of the plant, the shape of its leaves, the color of its flowers and even the shape of the capsule. The mature Poppy may vary in height from 12" to 4'. It may have either a hairy or a smooth stem. Most wild poppies will tend to the shorter end of the range of height, because since they are not being cultivated in densely-packed plots as protection from the wind's crushing influence they must huddle nearer the ground to survive. I have also noticed, most unscientifically, that the wild poppies I've seen seem to have smooth stems.

The capsule, which forms after the flowers drop away, comes in many shapes - elongated as an egg, globular in a spherical sense, a flattened spheroid, and so forth. Capsules in cultivated varieties range from the huge to the relatively small, with wild varieties tending to be small; again probably because the wind will readily knock over a top-heavy plant. So the wild Opium Poppies one is likely to encounter will probably have capsules not exceeding 2" maximum diameter.

The root of the plant is a single fusiform main root with a few lateral branchings near the soil surface (another factor in the plant's liability under strong wind conditions.) The stem normally shows from three to seven branchings, though this number can run much higher, and these branchings are slightly waxy in appearance often yielding a somewhat bluish tinge of color. The lower leaves are broad, spatulate and have irregularly indented margins and are usually hairy along the midrib on the underside, while the upper leaves are small and have deeply indented margins, and are attached to the stem by what appears to be a ring of fiber which surrounds the stem. The flowers may range through the entire spectrum that is, be any color, and mixtures of color often appear on the same plant. They have four broad petals. There are from one to two hundred stamens which are arranged in circles usually numbering five. The stigma is a flat, star-shaped disc, and the pods contain from several hundred to several thousand seeds, which may also be of any color, though all seeds within any given pod are the same color, not necessarily the same color as the flowers.

Cultivation of the Opium Poppy

How you cultivate the Poppy will depend to a great extent on where you live, because climatic conditions, soil composition and moisture/dryness cycles play an important part in determining cultivation variables. Consequently, there is no single overview of cultivation which could be effective for cultivators living in such diverse places as, say, Southern California and upstate New York. So, what we'll do in this section is take a look at several parts of the world where the Opium Poppy either is or was grown for an alkaloid harvest, and by doing so we'll be able to cover the range of conditions which US cultivators might encounter in different parts of this country. From this discussion we'll move to a consideration of the various harvesting and processing techniques which are practiced in a number of places; these techniques, being far less dependent on environmental variables, may generally be accepted or rejected by the individual cultivator regardless of where located.

Climate and soil considerations in the countries discussed below correspond reasonably well to those which might be encountered by a prospective cultivator living anywhere in the northern and central tiers of states in the US, areas characterized by regular seasons which include winters with snow and soil types ranging from depositional (rivers and glacial) through rock-derived.

Country-Specific Cultivation Techniques

Bulgarian Cultivation Techniques

In a country like Bulgaria, where winters can be quite cold and where heavy snows are the rule, the Opium Poppy is best sown in the autumn for, while it is capable of withstanding very low temperatures if insulated by a blanket of snow, if it is sown in the spring there is a far greater chance of disruption of its cycle of water requirements by a too-wet late summer. The Opium Poppy grown under temperate-zone seasonal conditions requires substantial moisture during germination and vegetation but, once the plant has come to flower, the requirements shift to a relatively consistent dryness. A plant sown in the spring, therefore, will face both a potential dry spell during summer, at the height of its vegetative growth, and a wet season in the late-summer, early-fall as it is coming to fruition.

Cultivators who live in areas which experience cold winters in combination with good snowfall should, therefore, sow the Opium Poppy in the fall of the year. If, on the other hand, one lives in an area which experiences cold winters but is generally very sparse in terms of snowfall, thus depriving the Poppy of insulation against the cold, it will probably be necessary to revise this planting schedule and sow in the spring, resorting to extensive irrigation during the dry summers and praying that any fall rains which may normally be expected in the area will hold off until after harvest time.

During sowing, moderate temperatures are most desirable, because in very hot weather the young plant is encouraged to grow far too quickly for its relatively fragile root system to develop to the point where it can support the weighty elongation of the stem and flower heads. The optimum temperature for germination of the Opium Poppy whose ancestors are of the northern temperate zone variety is 50°F, though it can germinate under an environment with an average daytime temperature of as low as 42° F. The young plants do well in an environment where daytime temperature's run in the mid-fifties and the nighttime lows do not fall below the upper thirties.

The above temperature considerations obviously apply to growing regions which are pretty well north - let's say roughly including all of Canada and some parts of the upper tier of US states. The meaning of these temperature considerations for growers in these areas is that they should not attempt to grow Opium Poppies whose seeds they have gathered from areas with temperature ranges substantially different from their own and, when the seeds of the right plants are sown, they should be planted with consideration to avoiding the heat of midsummer.

Once the young plants are well-established, even relatively low (though not hard-freeze) winter temperatures can be withstood, provided there is a good consistency to the snows. If one lives in an area swept by cold during the winter - temperatures down to and perhaps below freezing but without the benefit of snow, then there is little chance of becoming an Opium Poppy cultivator without engaging in greenhouse culture.

A general guideline to cultivators in the northern areas of this continent is afforded by the general rule that Bulgarian Opium Poppies were sown in the autumn just after the sowing of winter cereals.

On the question of which type of soil to choose, one finds that Bulgarian Opium Poppies are thought to thrive in any soil which is favorable to the cultivation of cereal crops. The soil should not be overly dense - that is, it should be sufficiently pervious to allow good percolation of moisture, because the Poppy does not easily take up moisture from the subsoil. The structure of the soil must be good, because the Poppy has a difficult time in holding its own against the force of the wind. The soil should be rich and also should be well-treated with manure or fertilizer. The experience of Bulgarian Poppy farm managers is that the best fertilizer regimen is to apply a good phosphorous fertilizer to the soil immediately before sowing, and a nitrogenous fertilizer in the mid-vegetative period.

Soil which is to be planted with the Poppy should be deep-worked several times in the period immediately preceding sowing, and attention should be paid to hoeing and thinning throughout the autumn, as well as in the spring after the snows have gone.

The seeds are planted at a rate of about twelve pounds per acre, and sowing is carried out by a variety of methods. Whatever the method, the seed, when sown, should lay at a depth of about 1/4 inch. Before sowing, the seed is treated with a fungicide; in the case of Bulgarian collective farms, a .25% solution of formaline is usually used, the seed then washed with water and left to dry in a windy, shady place. During drying, the seed is turned frequently to promote uniform drying. Seed sown in rows, as is the normal practice on these farms, is distributed so that one arrives at a distance of 12" between rows and, when the young plants are sufficiently well established (four to five weeks), thinned out so that there is approximately 5-6" between plants.

Balkan Cultivation of the Opium Poppy

Large-scale cultivation of Somniferum began in the former Yugoslavia in the mid-nineteenth century, and for many years it played an important economic role in the country. As late as the mid-1960's the Poppy continued to flourish in the east-central region of Yugoslavia, principally in the Vardar river valley, and most intensively in the districts of Stip and Titov Veles.

The climate in this region of Yugoslavia is characterized by a mild, wet winter with a swift seasonal changeover to hot, dry summers beginning in late May. The climate of this region corresponds roughly to that of the mid-atlantic, central and southern Appalachian mountain regions of the United States.

The Yugoslavian Poppy is a reasonably hardy plant, able to withstand winter temperatures as low as the low twenties for brief periods, particularly when it is protected by a good layer of snow. As in all other parts of the world, a cold winter without snow spells destruction for the Yugoslavian Poppy. Again, as elsewhere, the ideal climatic cycle is one which provides plenty of moisture through the fall, winter and early spring, changing over to hot, dry weather during the final phases of growth. The average annual rainfall in the opium region of Yugoslavia is 14-20", depending on location. This, too, corresponds nicely with the aforementioned parts of the United States.

Also as elsewhere, the Yugoslavian Poppy does best in light, well-structured but friable soils which are either naturally rich or which have been well-manured. Where natural fertilizers are available they are used generously; when chemicals are used, they are worked in at the rate of 300 pounds of nitrogenous fertilizer and 600 pounds of superphosphate per acre. The Yugoslavian Poppy is felt to grow best at altitudes not exceeding 2500 feet above sea level.

The Poppies are sown here in late September, as soon as the fall rains have begun. Sowing takes place in rows consisting of from two to four furrows, each furrow separated from the other by 8-10", and each row of furrows separated from the next by about two feet. From six to ten pounds of seed per acre are used, and the seed is placed in the furrows which are then harrowed so that the seed lies at a depth of about 1/4"• To make sowing easier, Yugoslavian farmers usually mix seed with clean sand in a ratio of 1:2 seed to sand. When well mixed, this mélange of seed and sand not only promotes uniformity of distribution of the seed but also adds a stabilizing element of the soil. As elsewhere soils which are too heavily laced with clay or which are prone to becoming waterlogged are avoided.

Along about mid-February the plants are thinned so that they are spaced 3-4" apart, and all grass and weeds are pulled up. The rows of poppies are then banked slightly. A second weeding and banking takes place about a month after the first. The poppies begin flowering around the first of May.

Turkish Opium Poppy Cultivation Techniques

For many years Turkey was one of the great Opium Poppy growing regions of the world. Only very recently, under pressure from the U. S. government, were the Turkish peasants deprived of the right to grow this traditional crop. One can't really quarrel with the need to limit the flow of Opium to the processing centers where heavy drugs are made in France and Latin America -there is, after all, no good which can come of the nasty white shit made from the juice of the poppy. One only wishes that people who use drugs were uniformly able to do so in moderation, and to use the drugs in their natural form - raw Opium, in the case under discussion. Were international contraband traffic confined to the natural drugs - like Opium and Cannabis -instead of proliferating into crap like heroin and morphine sulphate, perhaps there would be less concern with the consequences of drug use and therefore a more balanced perspective on drug production in countries like Turkey.

Be all that as it may, the would-be cultivator of a few backyard poppies for moderate home consumption of raw Opium can learn a lot from examining the techniques of the Turkish cultivator. The climate of the opium regions of Turkey corresponds nicely to that of a great deal of the United States, notably the mid and south-west, and the central and southern Pacific coast, including also the plateau regions of the central west - New Mexico, Colorado, Utah and Nevada.

So much good, straightforward information is available from the Turkish Soil Products Office (or, rather, was available until recently) that I will simply quote from a collection of these helpful hints to growers rather than paraphrase the information.

Steps in Cultivation

SOWING

A. General observations

A good farmer always chooses good seeds. He refrains from incision a certain number of the well-developed principal capsules; and after the seeds have ripened he collects these capsules and keeps them separate until the sowing season.

These rules should be observed by all growers, but this is not always done.

B. Time of sowing

It is always advisable to sow poppies as early as possible, as the plants can then develop, in the case of winter cropping, before the winter frost, and, in the case of spring cropping, before the dry season.

Poppies may be sown in the autumn or spring. In Turkey they are mostly sown in the autumn. Between 60 and 70 per cent of the poppies grown are winter crops. The time of sowing varies, according to local climatic conditions, between September and December.

For spring crops, sowing time varies between February and April.

The plants sown in autumn are usually more robust and healthier and give better yields. In areas, however, where the winters are severe but without snow, autumn cropping is not possible.

Very often the grower divides his field into three parts and sows it as follows: one third at the beginning of autumn: one third at the end of autumn; one third in spring. Thus, part of the harvest is always to some extent guaranteed.

The first lot, for example, may suffer from drought at the beginning of autumn, but once that period is past the winter frosts (especially if there is snow) and the summer droughts can do no further harm.

As regards the second lot, too early winter is dangerous, because the young plants may then be easily destroyed.

The third lot has nothing to fear from frost. Its only enemies are the spring droughts. As a spring crop it never gives very good harvests, but an average volume is ensured provided the drought is not severe. When the sowings are staggered in this way the work of thinning-out, weeding and incision is similarly staggered. The grower can carry out the work in one part of the field after the other with the assistance of the members of his family and without having to use hired labor.

C. Method of sowing

The small farms on which the poppy is grown have almost no machinery. Moreover, drills for sowing poppies are unknown, and the ordinary machines for cereals cannot be used for the small poppy seeds.

The poppy seeds are either sown broadcast or in rows, the broadcast method being the more common. In most cases the seeds are sown broadcast without dividing up the field, but sometimes the field is divided into strips of about two metres wide with a space of 40 centimetres between each. When sowing by rows, furrows from about 60 centimetres apart are made. The seeds are dropped in them and afterwards covered by means of a harrow.

Before sowing, the seeds are mixed with sand in a proportion of from two to five times their volume. In certain areas it is also customary to moisten them before sowing.

A quantity of from 3 to 5 kilogrammes of seed would be sufficent per hectare if drills were used. The row method takes from 5 to 15 kilogrammes and the broadcast method about 20 kilogrammes. If the field is not well prepared, some growers use up to 25 or even 30 kilogrammes of seed per hectare.

If the broadcast method of sowing is used, a large proportion of the seeds remains uncovered or go too deep down and are thus lost. That is why the quantity of seeds used with this method is so great.

The seeds should not be buried deeply, or the rudimentary shoot will be unable to develop. The layer of earth covering them should not be more than 1 to 1.5 cm. deep.

If the soil is dry, one must wait for rain or, if possible, irrigate the field before sowing. If the field is irrigated after sowing the seeds may easily be carried away by the water.

D. Various stages of growth

The germination of the poppy seeds usually lasts from two to three weeks. Seeds sown in late autumn or early spring may in cool weather require up to six weeks for germination.

Three to four weeks after germination the first four leaves of the plant are formed.

In spring, as soon as it is warm enough for growth to be resumed, or, in the case of spring crops two or three weeks after the development of the first four leaves, the stem begins to form. The plant reaches full development in from 40 to 60 days. During this first period of growth the poppy needs moisture.

The flowering season varies according to the region, altitude, situation of the field and variety of poppy. For example: at Aydin, flowering occurs at the end of April or beginning of May; at Afyon it occurs in the second half of May; at Corum and Malatya it occurs towards the end of May or the beginning of June.

Flowering takes place during the day, the flowers hardly ever opening on rainy days and almost never during the night. A flower remains open for thirty to forty hours, after which it begins to wither. A field will remain in flower from four to five days.

Often the pollination is direct and in the remainder, indirect. Thus, the poppy is also fertilized by neighboring plants.

After the petals fall-the capsules continue to grow for a fortnight longer. Then comes the right time for incision.

E. Work to be done during growth period

During the first period, the growth of the Opium Poppy is slow, and, in particular, if the field has not been carefully prepared, weeds may easily smother the young poppy plants, and prevent them from developing. In addition they may impoverish the field in moisture and nutritive material.

Thinning-out and weeding are not usually done in autumn except when the seed was sown very early, or when, after a rainy autumn, the weeds begin to invade the fields before the winter sets in. If, however, it is not desired to do thinning-out or weeding during the winter, the weeds can simply be uprooted by hand. In spring, on the other hand, thinning-out and weeding should be done for winter crops as well as for spring crops as soon as the weather permits. It is after the first weeding that the poppy plants recover their strength.

Thinning-out is always done after the first four leaves are formed. The superfluous seedlings are removed so as to leave about fifteen plants per square metre (25 cm. between the plants) if the seeds were sown broadcast, and about 10 to 15 cm. between the plants if the seeds were sown in rows. Plants which have been left too close together do not grow well and remain small. They yield small capsules and the work of incision and collecting is also more difficult.

If the plants are too far apart they cannot support one another during wind and rain, and there is a danger that they may be blown down.

Weeding should be repeated two or three times, or oftener, if possible.

In the case of line sowing the first weeding may be done with a weeding plough.

The second weeding should be accompanied by ridging of the earth.

When the stems are formed it is necessary, in the case or varieties which produce numerous capsules, to thin out the capsules, or they will remain small and the harvest will not be so good.

Turkish closed-capsule poppies do not form many capsules, but even here good growers sometimes remove the secondary capsules in order to allow those remaining to develop and grow larger. The growers are thus able to save a lot of labor during the harvest.

F. The enemies of the poppy

The poppy-plant has many enemies during the various stages of growth. The following are the more important: (a) Mildew (Perenospora arborescens) attacks more especially the poppy leaves, on which it forms white spots. In time the leaves shrivel up, wither and die; (b) A plant parasite (Orobanche papaveris) battens on the poppy by using its suckers to absorb the nutritive matter in the plant; (c) Rodents like field mice or insects of the beetle type and their larvae do damage to the leaves and roots; (d) Before the campaign against locusts was successful, they were also an important enemy of the poppy.

Indian Opium Cultivation & Preparation Techniques

The Opium of Patna-Garden has been, over time, judged to be the superior quality Opium of India, by virtue of its quality measured by Morphia content, subtleties of appearance, taste and odor, and by virtue of the yield per capsule. Any prospective cultivator contemplating a seed-collecting trip abroad could not do better than to visit this region in hopes of finding the seminal energy for his prospective crop.

The Patna district is located in Upper Bengal, bounded by 25°-25°41' north latitude and 84°36'-86° east longitude (Greenwich). It lies along the southern bank of the Ganges, and the greater portion of the district is subject to annual inundation from this great stream. The amount of land which is suitable for Poppy cultivation, thus, is limited to the higher ground, principally that land surrounding the ancient town of Patna itself.

There are three major Opium cultivation districts near Patna. Two of these are located in the Ganges flood plain to the northwest of Patna. The alluvial soil of these areas is a mixture of sand, clay and topsoil laid down by the occasional high crests of the river in flood; their color is grayish, and they have good permeability. The third area directly surrounds the town of Patna, and is a peculiar soil called Karah-panee by the townspeople. This gray soil is a mixture of sand and topsoil with a strong but light clay binder, and is strongly impregnated with saltpeter and a residue of calcium carbonate. It is considered the best soil in the world for Opium Poppy growing. This soil yields an average of 35 pounds of processed opium per beegah, a growing plot comprising 1200 square feet. The temperature at Patna ranges from a high of 102° in June to a low of 48° in December.

In late October, following the last of the monsoon rains, the cultivation of the Poppy begins. The chosen land is turned to a depth of a foot. Upon occasion a mulch of vegetable matter, manure and house sweepings is worked in with the turning of the soil. The land is then divided into squares of earth 6'x4', with mounded earth 18" thick and 12" high separating the plots. The seeds are broadcast sown around the first week in November, and are raked gently under.

When the young plants are 4-6" high the first post-planting weeding takes place, and the process is repeated weekly thereafter. Toward the end of March the plants have reached their maximum height and are approaching maturity, having bloomed and lost their flowers around the middle of the month. The days are warm, in the nineties, and nights moderate, in the seventies, with heavy dews in the early morning hours.

The Critical Phase and Its Signs

The poppy field reaches fluorescence in a relatively coordinated fashion. Within four or five days of the appearance of the first fully open flowers all of the poppies in the field will bloom. Then, within a very short space, all of the petals will drop away. There is very little difference between the blooming of autumn or spring planted poppies, the spring-planted fields blooming only a few weeks later than the fall this, of course, is due to the winter dormancy of the fall-plantings.

The critical phase for Opium collection is reached about two weeks after the petals have fallen away. There are a number of indicators which experienced cultivators watch out for. The upper part of the heretofore light to medium green stalk begins to darken. The lower, broad spatulate leaves begin to yellow. The capsules, which have been kind of spongy-soft until now, harden noticeably to the touch, and most varieties will undergo a color shift from light green to a darker green with a brownish tinge; others will go from a light green to a dull metallic blue sheen. When one presses the capsule it is possible to detect the firming-up of the inner wall of the pod.

The real giveaway for the exact time for harvesting can be detected by watching the ring at the base of the capsule where the petals were joined. This ring will usually mirror the color of the capsule itself during the period after the petals have fallen; it may be a bit lighter green. Suddenly, however - within a single day - the ring will darken dramatically, becoming anywhere from a coffee-brown to a dark black. This is the sign which growers must wait for, and must not miss. Each day one waits after the appearance of this dark ring will drastically decrease both the yield of opium milk and the alkaloid content of the milk which is given.

There are two great enemies of the grower at this critical phase wind and rain; also, heavy dew is very undesirable. The reasons for these environmental conditions being problems are probably obvious. A strong wind will dry the latex seeping from incisions in the capsule before it has a chance to escape the cut, thus blocking the excretion of any more milk. A rain will wash away the latex, and heavy dew will thin it out so much that it will run down the sides of the capsule and be lost onto the ground. Planting strategy is aimed at bringing the crop to harvest during a period when all conditions are most likely to be favorable for the incising of the capsules and collection of the milk; thus, the importance of calculating your planting times with an eye to the eventual harvest-time cannot be stressed enough.

Current Indian Opium Varieties

Here is a list of the major poppy varieties being grown in India today. You may want to use this as a guideline if you are going to order poppy seed online for your garden.

1. *Teyleah variety or Telia, Haraina, Hariala, or Herera*

   This is a favorite variety with many of the cultivators though far less generally grown than it deserves. For an early crop, it is certainly one of the most productive sorts. It has oblong ovate capsules with a pale, olive green color, without powdery coating

2. *Sufaid-danthi or Katha Bhabutia*

   This is one of the most generally cultivated of the several varieties grown in the agency, though as a rule less productive than the teyleah variety for early crop. It is, however, far superior to it for late cropping.

3. *Kutila, Katila or Kotila or Chansura, Ghanghabaha, Chirrah or Bhagbhora*

   The varieties are better than any of those ordinarily cultivated for withstanding hailstorms and high winds, because of their much reduced and narrowly segmented foliage of thick and dense texture. They also, better than any of the other common cultivated varieties, resist the blights to which all are more or less subject. The varieties will do well in a sandy loam. The capsules are oblong-ovate and glaucous. The latex is red at the time of lancing. Sometimes there are bristles on the flower stalks.

4. *Choura Kutila*

   This is also an excellent variety though less cultivated than any of those mentioned above. It differs chiefly from the last ones in having thinner and less narrowly and deeply cut foliage. It requires a strong and retentive clayey loam and more moisture than the other varieties.

5. *Kaladanthi, Karria, Damia, Kalidanthi, or Kalidandi*

   This is an excellent variety and more generally cultivated than either of the two last named. It is well marked by the peculiar bluish-black color acquired by the flower stalk soon after the fall of the flower. This is a less robust variety than any of the preceding. It produces, however, a great quantity of opium. It has a less protracted season than any of the other varieties and gives better returns as an early than a late crop. The capsules are oblong-ovate and glaucous, the latex slightly reddish at the time of lancing.

6. *Subza Kaladanthi or Haraina Kalidanthi*

   This is a new race of the preceding variety. This variety cannot stand heat and excess of moisture in the atmosphere or the soil. It is good as an early crop on light well drained soil. Later in the season, the heat becomes too strong, the capsules shrivel and lose their color, drying up prematurely and yielding little opium. It differs from the preceding varieties in having capsules of an olive green color.

7. *Kalidanthi Baunia*

    Same as Kalidandi but with smaller plants and produces more opium than the Kalidandi variety.

8. *Monoria*

    Produces a large amount of opium but requires a well manured soil of the strong clayey-loam sort. In light sandy soil it is less productive, the capsules are also smaller, of an ovate-oblong shape, and they are scarcely distinguishable from the common sufaid-dheri variety. It has large, roundish, ovate and glaucous capsules.

9. *Dheri-Danthi*

    This is a new race, derived from the common sufaid-dheri. It is much less subject to the common poppy blight than any of the old varieties. However, it does not produce much opium but its opium contains a high percentage of morphine. This is an important property aside from the comparative blight immunity. Its several good qualities recommend it for experiments on a small scale with a view to its selective improvement.

10. *Variegated poppy*

    This is another new race of the sufaid-dheri variety which is little affected by blights and pests. This important quality is attributable to the more highly oxygenized state of the tissues than that of the normal forms. It is quite possible that by experiment and selection it may be developed into a good opium producer.

11. *Sufaid-danthi Monoria*

    This is an excellent hybrid, very robust and producing large and uniform capsules of a roundish-oblong shape.

12. *Monaria Teyleash*

    This is also a hybrid which may become a good opium producer. It resembles its female parent Monoria in general appearance and form of capsule, while the texture of the capsule is quite the teyleash type, of a deep opaque green colour.

13. *Sandpha, or Dhadhua or Bhabhua*

    The plants are higher than any other variety with big capsules of roundish-oblong shape. This variety yields little opium.

14. *Sahbania*

    A variety grown in Eastern districts. It has long leaves with the two basal lobes falling down the leaf stalks. Capsules are oblong-ovate with a rough surface. Does not yield much opium.

The Madhya Bharat and Rajasthan poppy differ considerably from the Uttar Pradesh poppy. It has a straighter stalk, simpler stem, sharply toothed leaves, of much thinner texture and the usually red or purplish colored flowers, with fringed petals and rather large sized oblong or ovate-oblong capsules, crowned with broad stigmatic rays. The main varieties grown in that region are:

1. *Bhatphoria or Dhaturia*

   Average height of the plant 3 feet 6 inches. Capsules 3" x 2½" roundish elongated, light green. Poor opium yield.

2. Galania

   Height 4 feet or less. Flowers white with pink or dark pink border. Size of capsule 3" x 2", round, oblong and flattened a little on top. Color of capsule dark green. Yield more opium and less seed than the Dhaturia. Color of opium light brown.

3. *Hybrid of the above two varieties*

   Petals red and white. Often white only, but mixed also. Average height of plant about 4 feet.

4. *Ramzatak*

   Flowers white and red white in color. Capsules small and elongated, slightly flattened at the top. Size 3" x 2". Opium yield more and seed less in comparison to Dhaturia. Color of opium dark brown turning black.

5. *Telia*

   Flowers white, petals 2½" long, not furcated. Capsules elongated, light green and shining. Opium of a dark shade. Seeds white. Produces more seed than Ghotia or Chaglia.

6. Ghotia

   Petals 2¼", white or with pink border. Capsules round, dark green. Color of opium as in Telia. Produces less seed than Telia but more than Chaglia.

7. Chaglia

   Petals 2½", red or pink with white dots at the bottom. Major portion of the petal is colored. Shade of opium lighter than Nos. 1 and 2. Average yield highest of all. Seeds white.

8. *Kasturi or Tejani*

   Scarlet red flowers. Very poor yield of opium. Seeds red.

Incising and Harvesting Techniques in Four Countries

Each of the four opium-growing areas under examination in this section has somewhat different approaches to the process of incising and collecting Opium from the ripe capsules. We'll look at each area in turn.

Turkey

Once again, we can do no better than turning to a condensed version of the information provided by the Turkish Soil Products Office, which offers farmers the following advice:

The latex

When properly incised the stalks and leaves also provide latex, but incision of the capsule draws the juice upwards. The latex is between the epicarp and the mesocarp. The juice channels go from below, upwards. In order to gather as much juice as possible a great many channels must be cut. If incisions are made too deeply, however, the wall of the capsule will be cut right through and some of the juice will run down inside and be lost.

The latex accumulated on the outside of the capsules is white and liquid, but the moisture begins to evaporate immediately and the latex becomes more and more solid and its color more and more brown.

On warm, humid, calm nights, the latex emits such a strong odor that it is quite impossible to remain near a poppy field without contracting a headache or dizziness. The peasants who live near the fields often have to remain confined in their houses, even when it is excessively hot.

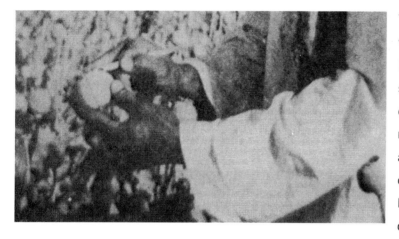

The incision of the poppy capsule is a very delicate and expert operation. Incisions which are too deep or too shallow or which are made too early or too late give bad results. The cut must be a shallow one but it must also be deep enough to allow the drops of latex to flow down outside. Incisions made in the middle of the day when the sun is shining give bad results and there will be hardly any flow of juice. It is therefore preferable to make the incisions either in the morning or in the evening.

When the incision is made in the morning, the opium is gathered in the evening. In such cases the opium is clear-colored and its qualities are regarded as superior by drug addicts who attach great importance to clear-colored opium. On the other hand, incisions made in the morning give a smaller yield. It is, therefore, now considered preferable in Turkey to make incisions in the evening, since color is of little importance in the case of opium intended for medical purposes. In such cases the opium is gathered the following morning. For this purpose, it is necessary to wait until the morning dew has disappeared. If the capsules are incised in the evening, the yield will be more abundant.

The latex takes from eight to fourteen hours, according to atmospheric conditions, before it solidifies and is ready for collection.

In case prolonged bad weather makes it impossible to observe these conditions, the grower will take advantage of a fine interval to incise the capsules and gather the latex in its liquid form.

The incisions are usually made with knives of various shapes, but there are also special instruments which are now increasingly employed. The best known of them is the so-called "Amasya" type. It has a broad end terminating in four to six lancet points, which have the advantage of not penetrating deeply and not piercing the capsule. The cuts made in the middle of the capsule produce most latex.

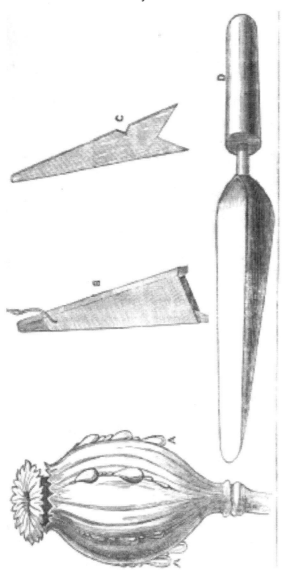

In a pamphlet published and distributed free by the Turkish Soil Products Office, the following advice is given to growers with regard to the incision:

[A] The capsule must never be cut all round. Spaces should be left unslashed between the extremities of the cuts in order that the capsule may continue to grow and the seeds ripen normally; [B] In order to obtain more latex, it is advisable to make several incisions (each covering a third or quarter of the capsule) at intervals of one day; [C] Incisions made on clear, sunny, calm days give the best results. In warm districts it is preferable to make the incision in the evening and in cool districts in the morning. It should be borne in mind that rain washes away the juice and that wind makes it fall to the ground; [D] Care must be taken to incise only the ripe capsules. This is why the farmer must go to the fields every day to select them.

Collecting the Opium

The latex which has caked on the capsule is raw opium. It is collected with a blade of some kind, as it may not be completely hardened, the peasants prefer to use an instrument that has a kind of gutter in which the semi-liquid opium accumulates. Very often a special copper tool is used which has the advantage of not scratching the epicarp and thus of preventing the admixture of vegetable tissues.

Where the grower uses ordinary blades the opium is usually gathered on poppy leaves.

The opium thus collected is deposited in a bowl or other receptacle, or, if sufficiently coagulated, the grower makes it into balls immediately.

The yield which is expected from a single capsule of Turkish Poppies varies considerably - it can run anywhere from 1/100 of a gram to 2/10 gram, depending upon a number of factors, not all of them having to do with the plant's genetic traits. For one thing, the yield per capsule is greatly affected by climatic conditions preceding the time of harvest - with hot, dry weather yielding the best effects. Also, on any given plant, whether or not the cultivator has eliminated many of the secondary capsules earlier in the growth cycle affects the yield of the primary capsules; and, even on an un-thinned plant, the higher, central capsules yield more opium than the outer, secondary ones. Then, too, the number of incisions made, the number of times the capsule is subsequently incised, all affect the gross weight yield of opium per capsule. How many times the capsule is incised over the course of the harvest varies with the intended use. In places where the opium is or was in tended for the pharmaceutical market, the capsules are only cut one time, because the first cut yields milk with the highest morphine content, and it is this which is important in determining the price received for the bulk raw opium. In areas supplying a smokers' market, multiple incisions are the rule, since profit lies in bulk, and since a lower morphine content, resulting from a mixture of the yield of second, third and even fourth cuts with successively lower morphine content makes a more suitable smoking product.

Preparing Raw Opium

This is a straightforward operation, without elaborate practice or ritual. The coagulated juice from the capsules is simply dissolved in water, placed in a container - often a bowl or deep tray - and covered over with a paper like rice paper, which breathes well and is opaque. The bowl is then set out in partial sun, and the heat slowly evaporates the water from the juice. After two weeks of this slow, steady drying the brownish mass which remains is the processed opium which is rolled and smoked throughout the world. The brownish liquid which sometimes remains in the bottom of the container is poured off, and can either be thrown away or used to adulterate Cannabis - this liquid, known as Passewa in the east, contains a very little amount of the alkaloids which give power to the opium gum

Bulgaria

Incision of the capsule occurs at the proper moment, judged by the appearance of the dark ring at the base of the capsule. The cut is single, penetrating no more than one to two millimeters deep, and is a horizontal cut encircling three-quarters of the capsule just below its greatest girth. The process of incising the plants usually begins about noon, and continues until six o'clock. On the following day, just after whatever dew has formed overnight has lifted, the process of collecting begins. On some collective farms in the early 1960's, an effort was made to collect the milk immediately after incision or, rather, on the same day, because research showed that by collecting the milk on the same day as the cutting, an increase of 36% in morphia content was obtained over what could be expected from milk left until the following day. Apparently there is a good deal of oxidation which takes place in the coagulating opium.

Former Yugoslavia (The Balkans)

There is very little remarkable about Yugoslavian incising and collection techniques. The capsule, at maturity, is incised with a single-bladed knife around the greatest circumference, and the cut is arrested when 3/4 of the capsule has been encircled, thus allowing the continued circulation of nutrients to the top of the capsule. The circulation of nutrient substances, including the latex, in poppy capsules is through a network of vessels which run vertically through the underskin. This is why with few exceptions the incising process in all parts of the world calls for circumferential rather than vertical cuts, in order to slice across the maximum number of latex- yielding vessels.

Yugoslavian workers make a point of walking backwards through the field they are incising, thereby avoiding the possibility of brushing against a newly incised capsule and thus rubbing off the first drops of latex. I've not seen or heard of this practice elsewhere, though it seems so logical I can't believe it's not in general practice.

Yugoslavian cultivators collect the yield on the day following incision, and there is only one incision made since the market for this opium is strictly medical. For some reason, Yugoslavian opium has a particularly harsh and unpleasant taste, and thus has no market for smoking purposes. Collection takes place with the standard sort of small blunt-edged knife, and the yield from each capsule is scraped into a little tin carried at the collector's waist. A person who is considered a good worker can collect between 200 and 400 grams of opium in a day's work, and the output per acre varies between 41/2 and 16 pounds, depending on the usual variables.

India

Patna growers depend on the same signs as do the Turks and all other growers to signal the approach of the time for incision - the color change into yellowing and, finally, the appearance of the thin black line. The incising of the capsule is done with a four parallel-bladed knife, with one pass of the hand from top to bottom of the capsule in a spiraling downward cut. The spiraling diagonal is said to prevent the loss of juice which would occur with a straight vertical cut, the latter allowing the juice to run to the ground, while the former gives the juice time to coagulate as it traverses the surface of the capsule.

The incisors enter the fields and perform their work between 11 a.m. and 3 p.m., so that the plants will have plenty of time to sweat in the sun, but early enough that the juice will coagulate enough to withstand the soaking of the early morning dew. In the morning following incision, after the dew has passed off, the gatherers move into the fields, and from the base of each diagonal cut, a tear of opium is obtained which in the case of Patna Opium, weighs about one grain. Thus each head of this superb plant yields four grains of high quality opium in raw state.

It is quite common for Indian cultivators to make four and five incisions, repeating the collection process on the day following each incision. As mentioned elsewhere, this process, and the resultant mixture of the yields of successive days will produce a product which is considerably greater in bulk than that produced by the medical opium producing areas but considerably lower in morphine content that that of such areas.

Your Seed Harvest

To obtain seed for next year's Poppy crop, allow the selected capsules to remain on the stalk until they are very dry. Do not incise these capsules. Seeds obtained from incised capsules are excellent sources

of oil, but are not thought to yield vigorous plants. In Turkey and India both, cultivators test the dried capsules for readiness by simply crushing the pod by hand. If it crumbles readily and is quite thin, then the grower sorts through the debris, picking out the seeds, and places them in a sealed container to be stored in a cool, dry place. The dried stalks and capsule debris, by the way, are usually saved for mulch for the next crop, since they are particularly rich in potassium.

A Quick Note on Degeneration

A lot has been written on the results of overdoing opium. I don't see this as a problem for those who grow a few plants - the chances are that none would long be able to get away with a whole field of Poppies no matter how botanically uninformed the locals might be, so that there would not be the material to overindulge, and in the second place I'm assuming that anyone growing Poppies will be doing so more as a self-sufficiency trip and perhaps as a way of gaining a bit of variety in drug experience, not as a way to get into some heavy habit.

There have been, upon occasion, some sensible things written about opium smoking which took the approach that if one must or will smoke opium, there is a right and a wrong way to go about it, and the right way is to keep one's body and mind close to earth as a matter of self-respect and self-interest.

Perhaps the most succinct little essay taking this approach comes from a British medical journal out of Singapore in 1908, which I will take the liberty of quoting for those who may be interested.

"We were shown in Batavia a most interesting paper upon the physical effects of Opium by Apotheker (Dr.) Haak, which explains many of the inconsistencies in the evidence upon the subject. He is of the opinion that the use of opium is comparatively harmless under the following conditions only: first, if the opium is smoked, secondly, if it is pure, thirdly, if the smoker is expert. That Chandu (high-grade opium) smoking is the least harmful form of indulgence in opium all are, I believe, agreed. As to the other conditions, Dr. Haak maintains that even Chandu smoking is always harmful unless the resins, gums and geetah in opium have been removed by the usual process of roasting and filtration and unless the Chandu so made is free from foreign organic substances, all of which gave an injurious effect, either because their fumes are actively noxious, or because their presence raises the temperature at which the Chandu is smoked.

On this last point he places great stress. He points out that Chandu smoking is merely the dry distillation of an organic substance, and that the substances which come over in the smoke vary widely according to the temperature at which the distillation is conducted - i.e. the temperature produced by the draw on the pipe. According to Dr. Haak, the more deleterious ingredients in Chandu are less volatile than those which are comparatively harmless, and the expert, well-to-do smoker who always keeps his Chandu as far from the flame as possible leaves dross which contains the maximum of harmful, toxic materials and thus gets his stimulation without great harm to himself, while the unskilled or poorer smoker, using much more heat, gets the maximum of stimulation out of a given amount of Chandu but at the same time absorbs into his system many poisons which the other smoker left in the dross.

Dr. Haak points out that the smoking of dross is particularly harmful because the dross has, in its previous distillation, lost almost all of its stimulating but comparatively harmless volatile materials which the original smoker enjoyed, and retains only the harmful ones whose effects, though similar in some respects to those of fresh Chandu, are also actively harmful.

It may be added that the confirmed dross smoker cannot get satisfaction out of pure Chandu, just as an absinth drinker cannot be satisfied with brandy. The typical Opium-sot or wreck is almost always a dross smoker; most Chandu smokers, particularly in the well-off communities, will do without rather than touch dross. And of course, dross eating is always far more harmful than even dross smoking though it is very common among those too far gone to tolerate indulgence in the time-taking ritual of smoking."

SECRETS OF AN OPIUM-GROWING MASTER

Arguably the world's foremost expert in opium poppy cultivation, both during his lifetime and since, was John Scott, a British colonial official given the task of establishing opium production for the Empire in India. Scott's book "Manual of Opium Poppy Cultivation" is extremely rare, and I haven't been able to turn up a copy at any price. However, I did manage to obtain a copy of the following report, which he wrote prior to his manual, and which contains almost all of the data and conclusions he used to write that Manual. I've left the Report largely unaltered except when changes were needed for clarity.

Anyone interested in traditional Indian methods of opium poppy cultivation, harvesting and opium preparation can have no better resource at hand than John Scott's work. In this section I have reproduced all of the most relevant and interesting information from this hard-to-find classic. I have eliminated a great deal of the minute details that so intrigued Professor Scott, and kept the information of most interest to today's medical opium growers.

Opium Fleet Descending The Ganges On The Way To Calcutta
An opium fleet of native boats conveying the drug to Calcutta. The fleet is passing the Munghyr Hills, and is preceeded by small canoes, the crews of which sound the depth of the water and warn all boats out of the channel, as the government fleet claims precedence over all other craft. The timber raft shown in the sketch has been floated down from the Nepal forests, and will be used in making packing cases for the opium.

Finally, just in case you are inclined to think of government-controlled opium poppy cultivation as ancient history here is a page from the India Ministry of Finance home page from September 2010.

"The Central Bureau of Narcotics is headed by Smt. Jagjit Pavadia, Narcotics Commissioner. He is assisted by three Deputy Narcotics Commissioners, each in charge of the three opium growing States of Rajasthan, Madhya Pradesh and Uttar Pradesh. The Deputy Narcotics Commissioner is assisted by the Asst. Narcotics Commissioner and District Opium Officers.

For cultivation of opium, Govt. of India frames an opium licensing policy every year (1st October – 30th September). The policy designates the poppy cultivation tracts, the guidelines for issuing licences to different categories of cultivators, the area to be cultivated, and the minimum expected yield of opium in Kgs./hectare. Illicit cultivation of poppy is an offence under Section 8 of the N.D.P.S. Act, 1985.

During the months of February and March, the poppy capsules become ripe for lancing, after which collection of raw opium is made by the cultivators. All cultivators are required to weigh their daily collection of raw opium which is entered in the preliminary weighment records maintained by the Lambardar. This operation is conducted under the overall supervision of the staff of the Narcotics Department. Thereafter the opium is delivered at the weighment centres of the Narcotics Department, which also conducts tests for purity of the tendered opium. The Opium bags are then sent to the Opium Factories at Neemuch in M.P. and Ghazipur in U.P.

The District Opium Officer, with the assistance of the field and preventive staff, exercises control over cultivation and procurement of opium produced and undertakes preventive checks to prevent diversion of opium into illicit channels. In addition, there are Preventive Cells located at vulnerable points to undertake such checks.

The Govt. Opium & Alkaloid Factories (GOAF) are engaged in the processing of raw opium for export purposes and manufacturing opiate alkaloids, through their two factories viz. Govt. Opium & Alkaloid Works (GOAW) at Ghazipur (UP) and Neemuch (M.P.). The Products manufactured at GOAW are mainly used by pharmaceutical industry of India for preparation of cough syrups, pain relievers and tablets for terminally ill cancer patients. The two factories of GOAW were declared as Commercial Undertakings in 1970 and are running on commercial basis. The security aspects of these factories are looked after by the Central Industrial Security Force (CISF), a paramilitary force of the Ministry of Home Affairs.

The working of the Govt. Opium & Alkaloid Works (GOAW) is administered by a Committee of Management constituted and notified by the Govt. of India in 1970. The Additional Secretary (Revenue) of the Department of Revenue of Ministry of Finance is the Chairman of the Committee. An officer of the level of commissioner/Joint Secretary is the Head of the Organisation and designated as Chief Controller of Factories. The present incumbent is Shri Ajesh Kumar. The two factories at Neemuch and Ghazipur are managed by General Managers, who are of the rank of Addl. Commissioner/Director.

And now for Scott's essay:

EXPERIMENTAL CULTURE OF THE OPIUM POPPY
JOHN SCOTT, Esq.,
PRINTED AT THE BENGAL SECRETARIAT PRESS, 1877.

SECTION 1. The soils of the Deegah gardens: their state of cultivation

SECTION 2. The soil of the Meetapore garden & its state of cultivation

SECTION 3. The water used in irrigation: its special qualities

SECTION 4. The weather: its general characteristics, for the opium season 1876-77

SECTION 5. The sowing season and allotment of land to the several varieties of the poppy

SECTION 6. The germination of the seed

SECTION 7. The season of growth and condition of the crops

SECTION 8. The drug-collecting season and opium produce of the several varieties

    a. The Deegah garden production from local varieties

    b. The hill or Simla poppy

    c. Deegah; comparative results of plane surface and ridge culture

       d. Seeds from unlanced capsules: produce of the fifth unlanced race

       e. The Malwah varieties

       f. The European varieties

       g. The Meetapore garden produce

SECTION 9. Pussewah; its nature and origin

SECTION l0. The seed harvest; the selection of the capsules and storage of the seed

Section 11. The diseases and injuries of the plant as caused by parasitic fungi, insects, etc.

Land & Weight Measures

Throughout this essay you'll find some unfamiliar weights & measures. Here are some approximate translations into the Western Pounds & Square Foot systems

Land Area

1 Beegah = 14,800 Sq Ft (@ 1/3 acre)
1 Cottah = 720 St Ft (1/20 of a Beegah)

Weights

1 Maund = @ 15 pounds
1 Seer = @ 1 pound
1 Chittack = @ 1 ounce

REPORT OF THE EXPERIMENTAL CULTURE OF THE OPIUM POPPY FOR THE SEASON 1870-77.

Introduction & Summary of Findings

I first discuss the garden soils, their improvement within these few years, and their present fitness for opium produce: the weather having been so favorable for their tillage (which is mainly what they needed) since the removal of the last crop. I then analyze the differences in the quality of the water used in the irrigation of the crops and their respective fertilizing properties.

I follow this with a discussion of the weather peculiarities of the opium season, as shown by the monthly averages, etc., of the barometer, thermometer, and hygrometer; the atmospheric pressure affording a low average, and an unusually high degree of moisture — conditions unfavorable, as I have urged, to any copious exudation of properly elaborated milk-juice from the poppy.

I then pass on to the sowing operations and modes adopted, reasons for preferring ridge and furrow to the common native mode of plane surface culture, as also the apportioning of the land to the local, Malwa, and European varieties of opium poppy of which I had seed in store. The germination of the seed, the growth of the plant, and the general condition of the crops at the flowering stage are the subjects of the two following sections. I show how largely the cool sides of the ridges promote the germination of the seed and benefit the young plant, and explain the evils of the ordinary plane surface culture in *koeries*. I also show that the plant on ridges, relatively to that in koeries attains the opium-yielding stage earlier, which is a great advantage.

In section 8 I deal with the peculiarities of weather when the plant attains the drug- yielding stage, as also the absolute and comparative fertility of the several varieties under cultivation. I show how weather influences the secretion of the plant's opium juices, and that the past season was highly unfavorable not only to that process, but even to the exudation of the drug from the scarified capsule. The result was that I had not even from my most carefully selected varieties anything like the high average return I had anticipated from the fullness and regularity of plants on all my plots of the local varieties— old and new.

I early anticipated a failure with the Malwa sorts, as indeed also with those of European origin, though I was not at all prepared to find them one and all so extremely unproductive as they proved. Both Malwa and European varieties proved alike impatient to the excessive moisture in soil and atmosphere; never acquired any vigor, and were alike infertile, in opium and seed. On the other hand, from my improved local varieties I had very fair returns, as is shown by a comparison with experimental district results. These, I think, plainly show the superior drug-producing properties which has been attained by the selection from season to season of seeds from the most copious drug-producing capsules. The comparative results of my own experiments with selected seeds with those of corresponding samples and local seeds in six divisions of the Behar agency are tabulated and discussed in the 9th section of this report.

I point out various discrepancies in the results of the district comparative experiments with my selected seed and that of local origin, and give reasons from my convictions that the Assamese, who nearly one and all apparently undertake such experiments with the greatest reluctance, have from the first determined in their own mind that the selected seed shall be a comparative failure, and but for the careful supervision of the several Sub-Agents interested with the experiments we would have had a very general illustration of the quaintly described practice (as quoted by the Benares Agent in his summary of the experiments with selected seed from 1875-76 in the *Old Pindaree* thus.— "There came the settlement hakim to teach me to plough and to weed : I sowed the cotton he gave me, but first I boiled the seed." This extreme antipathy of the natives to all innovations on their old modes is most unfortunate as I am sure could the Assamese only be got to cordially adopt and practice the modes I have recommended the productiveness of the plant would he very greatly increased. The results, however, of the distribution of Malwa seed in 1871-72, and its utter failure throughout the agency, and that unquestionably from inadaptability to climate and soil conditions, increase their distrust in all experimental seed, so that if ultimately induced to try it they in the majority of cases, I believe, do so with a view to compensation, warranted or unwarranted, from Government— *vide*, for example, the report, of the Sub-Agent of Allegunge in the appendix.

In section 10 I have briefly treat of the nature and origin of that opium depreciating matter, Pussewa. There are reasons given for the assumption that the segregation of this substance in the normal opium fluids is due primarily to excess of moisture in the soil and the atmosphere, and this specially prior to, and immediately after, the flowering of the plant, which comprises, as I believe, the most critical period for the proper maturation of the opium juices, and to which unbroken sunlight is apparently indispensable. With a marked deficiency of the latter, and excessive atmospheric moisture, respiration in the first instance is greatly impeded, and consequently an undue accumulation of watery fluids in the plants, which of course prevents the proper maturation of the opium juices and sets up a segregation of the inferior matter called Pussewah. This was the case during the past season, in which I show that, relatively to the season of 1875-76, last season's opium gave off as one to twenty percent more Pussewah. For all this, however, the drug returns of all the local varieties compare favorably with those of last season, and thus afford positive evidence of their continued improvement as drug- producers.

The seed-harvesting process next occupies my attention, and is dealt with in the 11th section. I have explained the mode of selecting the capsules, the differences in the grades of fertility of the seeds, and shown that this system, if adopted by the Assamese, while costing a most trifling amount of extra labor, would be manifold by remunerative, as the alone practical mode of developing, increasing, and perfecting the drug-secreting system of the plant. In this, as in former reports, I give clear, positive, and substantial proofs of this in the annually increased returns of opium yielded by the most carefully selected seed-crops. They are far, however, from having yet attained the high and uniform standard of productiveness, which clearly they will attain by the continuance of these practical experiments for some time longer.

Lastly, I briefly describe the diseases of the plant and the injuries caused by its insect and other foes. I show that gangrene in a moist form was the only disease which caused any real damage to the crop last season, and this more especially, in the case of the European and Malwa varieties. Far more serious than this, however, was that functional derangement of the whole drug-secretive system, due, as explained, to excess of moisture and deficient sunlight, which in suppressing transpiration from the plant and consequently an undue accumulation of watery fluids, gave rise to a copious segregation of the opium juices in the form of Pussewa, thereby very seriously lessening the produce of pure drug. These more than any real disease were the depreciators of last season's opium crop. The poppy mould, though prevalent, only appeared in the fertile or spore bearing form, and did no apparent injury to the plant. In discussing this mould I show how its development is modified on the poppy by slight alterations in the juices of the latter, also the possibility of our being able to rid the poppy of this its most destructive foe by such chemical applications to the soil and the plant as are likely to affect detrimentally the juices for the mould. The same mode of treatment, will, I doubt not, be found applicable to the potato and its mould, as indeed to all of the many other of our agricultural and garden plants affected by this class of parasitic fungi which infect the inner tissues. As I have elsewhere stated, we may thus also successfully contend with that cognate of the poppy mould which causes the muscardine of the silkworm. With the probability, then, of attaining these results, experiments would be ill-spared considering the high importance — agriculturally and commercially— of the products in question.

I will now only add that in illustrating and discussing these varied subjects I have not, I fear, made all so clear as might be desirable, though I am well convinced that future observations and experiments, yet so much required, will but confirm the views I have advanced in regard to the improvement of the poppy as a drug-yielder and modes of affording it a certain immunity from the blight mould. The work deputed me, I may explain, was in the first instance quite new to me ; I had everything to learn and observe, subsequently to consider and work out by experiments the best mode of attaining the objects in view. All this has occupied me for five successive seasons, and has of course occasioned a considerable expenditure, but still I think I may fairly claim the merit of having shown by practical experiments that the poppy — even as has been shown in the case of so many other products of the field and the garden - under careful selection will largely increase its productiveness. That, moreover, by simple, practical, and I do not doubt inexpensive, chemical applications to the soil or the plant we may free the poppy from that mould blight which periodically affects and quickly destroys the crops. These results, then, I think, fairly compensate for the time and expenditure, when the nature and peculiarities of the duties are fully considered. Reflecting thus on the progress that I have already made in both these important objects, it would be a great regret to me should Government discontinue my experimental works at their present interesting and encouraging stage. I do hope, therefore, that the Member in charge will recommend their continuation in the Deegah and Meetapore gardens for some time longer.

I particularly wish to show what these gardens are capable of returning by apportioning in future the whole to my improved local and the most productive of my new varieties. The results returned by the

Assamese and forwarded to me by the Agent are most unsatisfactory, and even though in the present report I have shown the superiority of selected as compared with unselected seed, I hope that I may be allowed to continue the garden experiments, as having a real and hearty interest in them, and thus naturally anxious to afford clear, practical, and satisfactory demonstrations of my views.

Section 1: The Soils of the Deegah Gardens: their State of Cultivation etc.

The soil in the Deegah gardens, though comprising an area of about 40 beegahs only, is very varied, and presents at least three well-marked varieties. Two of these appear to be especially well suited to the opium poppy, and fortunately comprise more than three-fourths of the area; the third variety, however, with a little management as regards irrigation and manuring, is also very fairly productive. I will briefly note the physical characteristics of these varieties. First, a pale grayish brown sandy loam, showing by analysis about four per cent, of iron oxide and a fair percentage of lime, potash, and magnesia. The bulk of it consists of sand in a finely comminuted state. The secondary basic component is a stiff plastic clay, which binds all together, and presents a uniform, fairly retentive, and upon the whole easily cultivable and productive soil. Secondly a sandy loam of a pale brownish color. It differs chiefly from the preceding in containing a smaller quantity of clay, and is thus less retentive of moisture and of course more expensively cultivable in dry seasons, as requiring irrigation more frequently. It is considerably richer than the other in the organic elements— carbon, nitrogen, phosphorus etc. and is thus somewhat the more fertile in so far as relates to the poppy. It is uniformly and finely comminuted (consisting largely indeed of an impalpable dust when dry), very friable, and of easy tillage. Hitherto the bane of both gardens at Deegah has been their infestment with the strong, deeply penetrating "kash" grass (Saccharum spontaneum) and that even more baneful and difficultly eradicable "moothoo" {Cyperus hexastachyus).

I need scarcely remind the reader that these lands, for many years prior to their being taken up for the experimental cultivation of the opium poppy, had been utterly uncultivated. They were thus quite overrun with the above strong rooting weeds, and have been brought again into an arable state at some considerable expense. In June 1873 they were first made over to my charge for the experimental culture of the poppy; so that they have now been under cultivation for four consecutive seasons. It is therefore scarcely necessary to remark here that, in so far as relates to the production of opium, they were then anything but suited (everyone at all acquainted with poppy culture knows well the disadvantages of newly broken in, or reclaimed land), though of course less so as regards mere seed production, as it was then very generally assumed that plants producing a minimum of opium do, on the other hand, yield seeds from which a more abundant opium-producing progeny will spring.

This I have shown to be quite a mistaken notion, and I need not dwell further on it here.

The lands from year to year, under the system of tillage adopted— expensive as it may, and indeed has appeared, to those unacquainted with their condition — have thus been gradually ameliorated, and are now really fairly well suited to the produce of a highly productive plant.

The continuation of the experiments is thus, I think, especially desirable on those lands of which I have now acquired a practical familiarity in so far as regards their general cultural characteristics.

The two soils above described comprise nearly the whole of the lands under culture at Deegah, the third variety being represented by small interposed patches of a few cottahs. This is a rather stiff sandy loam of a pale chocolate-brown color, becoming considerably darker in tint when wet, forming a thick plastic mud with water, and baking very hard when dry. It is more highly impregnated with iron than either of the above, and under drought presents many small patches of a yellowish red tinge, which well indicate its presence. In ordinarily dry seasons, with a liberal application of lime before the end of the rainy season, this soil is a fairly good producer of opium; on the other hand (from its highly retentive properties), in moist seasons the young crops are very liable to injury, and the ultimate drug produce scanty, low in consistence, and of a dark color. It is thus altogether less adapted to the poppy than either of the others; but fortunately, as above observed it occupies a very small area in the Deegah gardens.

Section 2: The Soil of the Meetapore Garden: it's State of Cultivation.

The main portion of this garden consists of a fine sandy clay of a grayish brown color, acquiring a darker tinge when wet forming a plastic mud when saturated, caking and shrinking considerably when dry. The total area of this garden is about 14 beegahs of which the above variety of soil occupies about three-fourths. Mechanically, as being finely and uniformly comminuted, it is well adapted to poppy culture; but unfortunately, under the exhaustive system of native culture, which appears to have been practiced prior to my taking over the lands for opium experiments in 1873, the first season's opium produce was very poor.

I have since considerably improved them by frequent tillage, applications of green and dry organic manures, and various mineral matters. They have thus been increasingly productive until last season, when, owing to the excessive moisture and the naturally retentive character of the soil, the plant neither acquired its usual vigor, nor did it afford anything like the normal quantity of pure drug, though there was really no apparent deficiency in the crude collections.

This I will, however, have occasion to treat of in a subsequent section.

With a matrix of sand and clay the above soil naturally contains a fair percentage of lime and potash, and has been latterly well enriched with organic matters. I can scarcely doubt, therefore, that these lands, under their present system of close tillage, and without any further extraneous manurial applications, will afford a high return of drug next season if the weather is only ordinarily favorable.

The remaining portion of the Meetapore garden consists of a sandy loam of a dull reddish brown color. It also contains a considerable percentage of iron, with very small quantities of lime and potash, and scarcely a trace of organic matters. The first season's crops on this portion of the garden were miserable in the extreme. Latterly, by various organic and mineral manurial applications, with frequent and regular tillage, it has been much improved, and is now having an application of urinary matters, from the adjoining jail, which will no doubt have a highly fertilizing effect.

For experimental purposes, and particularly for observations on the diseases of the poppy, the Meetapore garden is a most excellent adjunct to that at Deepak as consisting of soils differing alike physically and chemically, and thus affording an opportunity for observing and studying the influence of soil and other physical conditions on any particular disease of the plant. This is of course one of the most important, as it is one of the most difficult, of the duties deputed me by Government. In the casual and annual reports which I have for the past four years submitted to the Board, I have explained the cause and nature of all the more serious and prevalent of the injuries and diseases to which the poppy plant is liable, and I have also suggested certain modes of treatment of a remedial and suppressive nature. As regards that most serious of all the diseases to which the poppy is liable — I refer to its periodical blight - it is most desirable that opportunities, such as I have lately had, should be afforded me some time longer, seeing that I have suggested views, as to the conditions favorable and unfavorable to its development, very different from any previously advanced. Subsequent observations all go to confirm me in their accuracy, but a much more extended series are requisite to fully establish them.

Section 3: The Waters used in Irrigation

The waters used for the irrigation of the plant in the gardens here, with one exception, are drawn from wells (varying from 25 to 30 feet in depth); the other is afforded by a tank on the ground, which, however, being only 15 feet in depth, is liable in ordinary dry seasons to be exhausted a month or more before the close of the poppy season. While it lasts, however, it is extremely useful, as possessing highly fertilizing properties from the decay of the abounding water plants. I thus use it in preference to the well waters on all the poppy plots to which I can readily convey it.

The waters from the several wells in the Deegah gardens vary much in their fertilizing properties; and this of course, as might be expected, mainly in proportion to their saline qualities. It is indeed interesting to observe that here as elsewhere in the great alluvial plain of the Ganges wells in proximity to each other do nevertheless yield waters of very different qualities: one may be soft and sweet, another hard and more or less perceptibly brackish. Examples of this are furnished by wells here, though less than one hundred yards apart. There is also in a native garden adjoining our Deegah lands a well so highly impregnated with fertilizing saline matters that the soil without other manurial applications has for many years yielded annually excellent crops of potatoes and onions during the cold and hot seasons, and another of Indian-corn, millets, or brinjals, during the rains. This water, I may observe, though differing materially, is only some fifty yards distant from one in my garden here: this affords a soft and sweet water of slight fertilizing value. In the Deegah waters lime and potash are present in larger quantity than any other minerals. They are very poor in soda, present but traces of ammonia nitric and phosphoric acid, and are wholly wanting in carbonic acid. The normal level of the water in our wells has been considerably lowered by the drainage, I believe, of the now nearly completed portion of the Soane and Ganges canal, which runs parallel with, and in proximity to, these gardens, as it joins the latter river. When finally opened, however, and a regular flow of water maintained in the canal, there will, no doubt, be a considerable rise of water in the garden wells.

This will be a great advantage to the lands for general arable purposes; but I much fear that from the highly absorptive and exceedingly retentive nature of the subsoil they will lose much sanitarily as a jail settlement, if ever thus re-occupied. It may indeed be objected to this view that the canal water as a rule will not at any time much exceed in level that of the adjoining river. This is quite true, but there is this important difference, that between the river frontage and the jail lands there lies deep impermeable strata of kunkur, whereas there is an unbroken communication of clayey loam and sand between the jail land and the canal. The mere question of proximity has thus little to do with the sanitary question above raised.

Section 4: Weather Characteristics for the Poppy Season 1876-77

To the opium culturists the weather is a most important element in all that relates to the ultimate outturn. A hailstorm for example, and that by no means a severe one, will ruin his crop; while a heavy rainfall between the period of scarification of the capsules and the collection of the drug will leave little or none for collection: so also are high or gusty winds detrimental during the opium season, as alike checking the exudations and reducing their normal consistency, so that by the wavy friction of the capsules one on another the drug is lost on the besmeared capsules. Moreover, as I have elsewhere shown, dull, cloudy, or rainy weather in all cases tends to reduce, not only the quantity, but the quality of the drug exudations. Indeed I believe that more than any other known vegetable product is opium affected by changes in the weather conditions at the period of its maturation and extraction from the plant.

The atmosphere throughout the past opium season was unusually moist, and the actual rainfall was also in excess of any of the four preceding seasons which I have had to do with opium. I would not of course have it understood that the annual rainfall was at all in excess: it was indeed under the normal average, though again considerably exceeding that of the preceding year. My remarks of course refer solely to the periods of growth and maturation of the poppy plant. I will, however, give a monthly statement of the annual rainfall at this station for the opium season 1876-77 (beginning June 1876 and closing May 1877), to which 1 will add the temperature, barometrical and hydrometrical conditions of the atmosphere from the germination to the maturation of the crop.

From the month of June to September, inclusive, the total rainfall at this station was only 27.68 inches: thus — in June, nil; July, 6.90; August, 10.3; and 10.44 in September.

In October we had light rains on the 1st and 7th, from which to the 18th we had daily lighter or heavier rain — in all 2.39 inches, from which to the end of the month the weather was hazy in the mornings, more or less cloudy during the day ; the prevailing winds light and varying from north to north-west. The monthly average difference of the dry and wet bulb thermometer was at 6 a.m. 1.80 and at 8 p.m. 8.27, the morning minimum being 0.50 and the day maximum 11.50.

In November the prevailing winds were light, generally more or less south by west in the morning and moving round to north during the day. We had a few light showers during the month — in all 0.50 of an inch ; the atmosphere, however, was moist, the monthly average difference of the dry and wet bulbs being 2.22 at 6 a.m. and 14.67 at 3 p.m., with a minimum difference of 0.50 and a maximum of 19.50. The minimum temperature was 43.2, and the maximum in the shade 88.5.

December, with no actual rainfall, was throughout characterized by an excessively moist atmosphere, hazy and foggy mornings, more or less cloudy during the day, with light westerly winds varying daily almost from south to north. The dry and wet bulbs indicated saturation for 15 mornings during the month, the average minimum being 0.56, the maximum 15.20. The lowest reading of the minimum thermometer was 40.20, the maximum in the shade 80.00.

On the 12th and 13th of January we had, respectively, the 0.40 and the 0.60 of an inch of rain, but the weather throughout was characterized by more or less foggy mornings, cloudy days, with light westerly winds varying daily from south to north. In the course of this month the dry and wet bulbs indicated saturation for 18 mornings and in no instance exceeded a difference of 1.00, the average being 0.43 for the minimum and 11.20 for the maximum. The minimum thermometer in one instance indicated 42.00, and the maximum in the shade was 85.00, that of the solar radiating thermometer being 144.6.

February, as all but inaugurating, and anyhow affording the bulk of last season's opium in the gardens here, requires a somewhat more detailed meteorological notice than any of the preceding months. — Well, first as to rainfall: the total fall was 1.02 inches: thus— 0.10 on the 4th, 0.48 on the 7th, 0.28 on the 8th, and 0.16 on the 22nd. The rain on each occasion was a smart shower of short duration, and, being accompanied with a brisk wind, caused considerable loss in opium, as I will subsequently show. Moreover, on eight mornings the hygrometer indicated saturation and only in one instance daring the month, with a brisk west by north-west wind, did it present a difference of 3.00. The minimum difference of the hygrometer for the month was 1.77, and the maximum 11.64. The monthly average of the minimum thermometer was 41.73, of which the minimum, reading was 34.2; the average maximum in the shade 74.24, the highest reading 84.5. The solar radiating thermometer gave as a maximum 150.5, and a monthly average of 134.13. The barometer was low throughout the month; the average at 6 a.m. 29.917, the attached thermometer 61.00; at 12 A.M. 29.986, the attached thermometer 65.30; at 4 p.m. 29.914, attached thermometer 65.6; and at 6 p.m. 29.96: attached thermometer 64.8: the mean average pressure from the four daily observations being thus 29.918, the average of attached thermometrical readings 64.17. The prevailing winds were light, west-by-northwest; the mornings usually hazy, the day cloudy and fine. The effects of the low average pressure of the barometer on the exudation of the drug will be illustrated by a series of observations in a subsequent part of this report.

The collection of opium from the various local and other Indian varieties was completed before the end of March, the meteorology of which I will now notice. The rainfall amounted in all to the 0.8 of an inch, of which 0.5 fell as a sharp heavy shower on the 16th, the remainder in light showers on three other days. Notwithstanding this light rainfall the atmosphere was still unusually moist; the hygrometer occasionally indicating saturation in the morning, and a monthly average difference of 2.64 only, with a maximum average for the day of 14.57! The barometer was lower than usual, the average for the month at 6 a.m. being 29.932, the attached thermometer 69.0; at 12 a.m. 29.942, attached thermometer 80.0; at 4 P.M. 29.787, attached thermometer 78.90; and at 6 p.m. 29.788, attached thermometer 77.40: thus giving an average mean pressure for the four daily observations of 29.798, the average of the attached thermometer being 71.77. The lowest reading of the minimum thermometer was 45.0, the monthly average 54.28. The maximum thermometer in the shade, with a monthly average of 89.33, was once only so high as 98.0; while the highest point of the solar radiating thermometer was 159.5, and the average for the month 144.80. The wind was light, chiefly west-by-north-west; the mornings hazy, and giving place to light clouds.

In April the European varieties (which attain maturity considerably later than the local sorts of poppy) alone continued to yield a little drug. The mean temperature advanced considerably this month, with an increase likewise of barometric pressure and a drier atmosphere. The weather was very favorable for the maturation and collection of the capsules, which, together with the clearing the poppy-haulm or stalks from the land, were the main works for the month. There was no rain during the month, and the minimum average difference of the hygrometer was at 6 a.m. 6.99, and at 3 p.m. 21.66. The monthly average of the minimum thermometer was 67.30 that of the maximum 96.82; and that of the solar radiating thermometer 154.75, the maximum indication of which for the month was 168.50.

April may be said to have completed the poppy harvest; the only operations left for May being the clearing, sifting, and storing of the seeds. For such works the month was upon the whole rather unfavorable, we having no less than 3.33 inches of rain in this usually dry and hot month. Of the total fall we bad 1.73 inches in light occasional showers; the remainder, 1.60 inches, on the 19th and 20th, accompanied by a brisk easterly wind. Again, on the 28th instant, with a gusty and strong north-westerly wind, which sprung up suddenly about midday, we had a full of rain of the 0.63 of an inch. The gale came on quickly and unexpectedly, and unfortunately my solar radiating thermometer, though well secured, was blown from its stand and broken. As above remarked, the month was by no means favorable for seed storing, from the unusual moistness of the atmosphere. Thus, though usually a drier and hotter month than April, we find that, irrespective of the actual rainfall, the hygrometer indicated an excess of 4.97. The minimum average difference was 4.38, the maximum 91.10. The monthly average of the minimum thermometer was 73.66, that of the maximum in the shade 101.70 ; while that of the solar radiator was from the 1st to 27th inclusive— when it was broken— 154.69 the maximum reading of which was 168.00.

With this month the opium season is fairly completed, and the lands cleared for next season's preparatory tillage, or for intermediate cropping, which the Assamese generally consider the more remunerative mode.

Section 5: The Sowing Season, and the Allotment of Land etc.

In the Deegah gardens the sowing commenced on the 5th of October, and was completed with some trifling exceptions — chiefly owing to re-sowings — by the end of that month. The soil and weather were alike favorable for sowing operations when I commenced them as above; but unfortunately, on the 8th instant, a heavy shower forced us to discontinue the works, and this was succeeded daily by more or less heavy rains until the 18th instant. This seriously injured the sown portion of my plots, as I will have occasion to show subsequently. From the 19th to the 31st, inclusive, we had no rain, and the soil being in an easily workable state the main-part of the sowings were completed, and the seeds afforded a sufficiently moist bed to effect germination without artificial irrigation. This of course is a great advantage, and especially is it so in the native mode of leveling the sown surface inasmuch, as failing germination from the natural moisture of the soil the subsequent artificial application of water will induce on the most friable of soils a most partial and irregular germination, and of course a poor, patchy crop the plants being largely confined to the shrinkage openings of the soil. By the ridge system these bad effects are avoided, and water may be at any time applied beneficially after the sowing of the seed, the only care necessary being to admit the water gently to the furrows, and avoid flooding the ridges, so that the latter may be moistened by absorption only from below.

The ridge system of culture has also a further great advantage over the native mode of plane surface culture, in affording shelter to the young plant from the rays of the sun. Everybody who is acquainted with poppy culture knows the injury caused to the germinating crops when fully exposed to the sun's rays, and well indeed is it exemplified by the distribution of the plants on the ridges. Thus, though the seed is sown first over the whole plane surface and equally diffused, it is a remarkable fact that while germination takes place rapidly and profusely on the north and cool side of the ridges, all is dormant on the south and sunny side; this being to the last, as a rule, as void of plants as if hand-picked. This, indeed, is so very striking that it is still a matter of surprise to me that the Assamese should not have long ago adopted the system voluntarily, seeing as he does season after season the major part of his first-sown plant all but confined to the cool sides of the compartment ridges. Blind, indeed, has he in this respect been to his own interest. Moreover, as I have elsewhere pointed out, the growth of the young plant is greatly promoted by the loose and open condition of the soil around the neck of the plant. Such favorable conditions for the growth of the young plant cannot possibly be attained by plane-surface cultivation, as shortly after germination occurs the seed-beds must be irrigated — flooded, indeed, is the better term under native practice; the soil then settles and soon forms a dry and baked surface, but slightly permeable to air, and it must so remain until the young plant has struggled on and attained sufficient size to permit the loosening of the soil.

In view of these several advantages of the ridge system, then, I largely adopted it in the gardens here during the past season. Indeed of the 52.5 beeghas forming the gardens under my charge I only, for the sake of comparison, had four beeghas under the native mode of plane compartments, the remainder being ridged.

Under this section I have now only to explain the apportioning of the land to the several varieties which I had in stock. With this view I arrange them under three heads— viz. Locals, Malwa, and European. Now the quantity of land allotted to the old local varieties, and the new ones which they have given rise to under culture here, was in all about 89 beeghas. To the Malwa varieties, under the impression (from the past season's, 1875-76, results) that I had now fairly well naturalized races, I allotted 8.25 beeghas. Lastly, for the European varieties, which last season had grown so vigorously and, as compared with the Malwa sorts, gave a fair return of drug, I allotted 5.5 beegahs. The drug outturn of these several allotments will be found in the section treating on the collection of drug.

Section 6: The Germination of the Seed

The time elapsing from the sowing of the seed to its germination is largely— indeed I may almost say wholly dependent on the degree of moisture in the soil. Thus, if dry and powdery, it simply will not germinate; so also when saturated with moisture, or at all sticky when pressed between the fingers. The minute seeds of the poppy will only give off their tiny germs when the soil has a degree of moisture sufficient to render it open and friable: they cannot otherwise free themselves, but simply die off piecemeal in a soil at all cloggy or soddened. Again, under favorable conditions of moisture and, of course, heat (say a soil temperature of from 70 to 75 and an average atmospheric temperature of, say, 85.00), germination will take place in from five to seven or ten days; whereas failing a sufficiency of moisture I have observed seeds lie quite dormant for 20 and even 80 days, and after a light fall of rain then germinate very freely.

As regards the germination of the seed in the gardens here for the past season it was singularly uniform, free, and rapid. From the sixth to the eighth day the germination was general on most of the plots; on the others, with two or three exceptions, from the tenth to the twelfth. Under the ridge system the young germs were most abundant, and everywhere confined to the north and cool flank of the ridges. The soil, moreover, contained sufficient natural moisture to complete germination> so that over the whole of the 48 beeghas under ridge culture no artificial irrigation was required until after the appearance of the young plants. There was thus a considerable saving in labor; and moreover in only two instances (and this was the fault of the seed, not the system) was re-sowing necessary, each ridge bearing a superabundance of plants. Indeed this was so much the case that in future, instead of allowing four seers of seeds per beegha I shall give only from two and a half to three seers.

Now, I have already stated that I had four beeghas sown on the native system of plane compartments. The plots thus treated alternated with others under the ridge mode, all being sown simultaneously) and of course similarly conditioned as to soil, moisture, &c. On the sixth day, however, after the sowing of these lands we had a shower of rain, which had the effect of highly consolidating the surface (causing it to crust and cake in drying), and so checked germination as to necessitate partial re-sowing of the four beeghas under the native mode. On the other hand the ridges suffered not at all, their northern flanks being covered with young plants by the eighth day.

The seed of the European varieties (of course the produce or last year's crop, 1875-76, in the gardens here) germinated in about the same time, and with two exceptions quite as freely as the common local sorts. The exceptions were in the case of a black-seeded French variety, and one of Italian origin. This was wholly due to the imperfect maturity of the seeds, however, as out of a quarter of a beegha or so of each sort only some half-a-dozen plants of each sprung up. Both plots were thus subsequently re-sown with Turkey poppy.

Section 7: The Season of the Plants Growth, and General Condition of the Crop

From the beginning of November, when the crops had generally germinated, until the beginning of February, when all had nearly reached the opium-yielding stage, the weather was moist and upon the whole highly favorable to vegetation. This was especially the case in the month of November and December, and so also in January, with the exception of two days4n which the plant was considerably injured: this was on the 12th and 18th of that month. On the former we had a thunderstorm with a sharp, heavy fall of rain, which was succeeded on the latter date by another heavy fall of rain accompanied by a strong gusty wind. This had the effect of partially laying, more or less, much of the crop in the more exposed places, and thus doing not a little damage. The more advanced portions of the crop naturally suffered most, and were thus less productive of drug than they would otherwise have been. Such and other local casualties often seriously deteriorate experiments in opium culture, and materially affect results when general comparisons are made with those of other and distant localities which have not been so affected. Than opium, during the season of collection, I know of no more critical, dainty or exacting crop, so susceptible is it to the particular weather conditions of the locality.

Weather of course, as we all know, is in India most local as to particular conditions, though none the less a component of what we understand as season; and therefore, in instituting comparisons in experimental and ordinary opium culture, it is but fair that the comparative data should be obtained within a circuit of a few miles, where all have been very similarly affected by weather conditions. Having regard only to the maximum produce of opium in its widely diffused cultivation under the two agencies, of course it is easy to see how disadvantageously my best selected seed crops, under uncongenial weather, may compare with others, in this respect, favorably conditioned, but of the ordinary unselected kinds. I beg, therefore, that the element of weather may be duly considered in all such comparative estimates. Moreover, I will confidently add that under any especially favorable circumstances by which the ordinary unselected seed has given a high return of drug a properly localized or acclimated and selected seed would have afforded still higher returns. The inapplicability of the selective principle in the case of the opium poppy was all well enough so long as it was groundlessly assumed that the opium juices were fully utilized, and indeed essential to the perfect development of the plant. I have, however, shown that there are no grounds whatever for any such belief; that, on the other hand, the milky juice of the opium poppy may be wholly extracted without in any appreciable way affecting either it's vegetative or reproductive functions. There can thus be no question as to the plant's susceptibility to improvement as a drug-yielder. The difficulty lies in getting the native culturist to adopt or practice the principle; and the only hope of overcoming this is by the zealous and hearty co-operation of the officers of the department — one and all of whom are, I am sure, sufficiently familiar with the modes in which all domesticated animals and plants have been improved to have any doubt as to the applicability of like modes to the opium poppy.

Under this section I have now only to treat of the general condition of the plant during the above season. This I will best do under the three heads of Local, Malwa, and European varieties. First, then, for the local sorts, old and new. The former comprise those more or less generally cultivated under the native names teyleah, sufaid-dherri, kaladanti, kutila, chaura-kutila, and moneriah ; and I had of new varieties — originated in this Garden: sabza-kaladanthi, subza-kutila, dursa-kutila, gunaguu-posta, meudar-danthi, and three mongrel varieties. The general appearance of the plant in November and December was most promising, the foliage being well developed and nearly all of a deep glaucous-green. The ridges were also very uniformly covered with plant. In January, however, when the early-sown set had nearly attained their full growth, I observed that I might with great advantage have spared many more plants in the later thinnings, the plants generally being but slightly disposed to give off lateral branches, and in this respect differing importantly from that raised from the ordinary unselected seed. From such seed we generally observe some six or eight well-developed capsules, and even as many as twelve when the plant is allowed space to develop itself. On the other hand, with my selected seed, which is nearly all from the central or primary capsule of each plant, there is strangely enough but little disposition to give off lateral branches, and very few indeed of the plants bore more than three lateral capsules: indeed I believe a majority of them only two. I consider this upon the whole an advantage, had I only been prepared for it and simply left, as I found I might, twice the number of plants. This I will of course do next season. In the case of the past season, I thinned out more than I otherwise would have done from the largely developed foliage and really crowded appearance of the young plants on the ridges — a result chiefly of the unusual high degree of moisture alike in atmosphere and soil. I thus anticipated a more than usual development of lateral branches as the plant became fully developed. In this, as I have shown, I was mistaken. One bad result of this was that the early-sown plant suffered more than it would otherwise have done by the strong gusty winds and rain which occurred here, as I have already stated, about the middle of January. This was especially the case with one of my new varieties — that called meeudar danthi, which is the most fragile of all.

The following varieties of the Malwa poppy were subjects of experiment. They have now been in cultivation in Behar for the past six seasons, and for five successive seasons in the gardens here. The plant from which the seeds of the different varieties were selected had really given a very fair return of opium in the past season — 1875-76, and I was thus induced, from the medical superiority of the drug as compared with the common local sorts, to occupy more land with them than I had hitherto done. The varieties were received by me under the following names: — Lukria, leela, gungajulee, and uggarya. From these I have raised a few mongrel sorts and picked out some natural varieties, all of which I have cultivated during the past season. The growth of all, however, was poor and stinted, and the drug returns of course most disappointing, as will be seen subsequently. One and all of the varieties germinated profusely. The first sowings, which occupied five beeghas, having been sown on the 6th and 7th October, were greatly injured by the daily successive rains following to the 18th. In spite of the rain the germination was no way impeded, all the plots having been ridged; the subsequent progress, however, was none the less unsatisfactory. As regards these I was first disposed to attribute their sickly condition to the heavy rains subsequent to their sowings and after their germination, but the later-sown crops of the Malwa race, which escaped these ultimately succeeded no better. I can thus only attribute the failure of the whole of the Malwa race during the past season to the high degree of atmospheric moisture.

I now pass on to the European races, of which I had the following varieties from seed grown in these gardens in the proceeding season 1875-76: the common Turkey, the Spanish, two varieties from Italy, and two of French origin. The germination of the Turkey and Spanish varieties was tardy as compared with the local sorts, but nevertheless profuse. So it was with one of the Italians and one of the French, while another variety of each of these altogether failed, as I have previously stated, apparently from imperfect maturation of the seed. In the case of the other European varieties, though they ultimately exceeded the local sorts, both as regards vigor and height, yet I am sure, plant to plant, they did not attain above three-fourths of the weight of that of the preceding season. As in the case of the Malwa race, last season was evidently anything but favorable to those of European origin. From the generally vigorous habit, however, of the latter I have hopes of raising some really good mongrels through intercrosses with the local sorts. I have several of these for trial next season.

It is now desirable that I should give a brief separate notice of the general conditions of the plant in the Meetapore gardens, as the above remarks have reference to that on the Deegah lands only. The difference in the general appearance or habit and vigor of the plant here as compared with that of Deegah was this season very striking, the former being altogether much less vigorous and spare in habit. This I can only attribute to excess of moisture in the soil, the Meetapore soil being of a much more retentive nature than that of Deegah, and moreover it has a further defect in having no natural surface drainage, so that the falling rains simply rest on, ultimately subside in, and are absorbed by the soil. There was thus much injury done to the Meetapore lands by the three inches or so of rain which fell from the 17th to the 18th of October. Prior to this fall a small portion of the land had been sown in ridges. The seeds germinated well in spite of the rain, but to the last the plants were spare and thin and quite wanting in their usual vigor. The plant sown after the rains of October succeeded better, but none of them attained anything like the vigor of the past and preceding seasons— I refer to those of 1875-76 and 1874-75.

From the prior results of previous season's trial of the Malwa poppies on the Meetapore lands I altogether discontinued them, the soil being plainly unsuited to them. I tried two of the European varieties, however, but these failed even more signally (as will be seen by the results recorded in the subsequent section) than did the Malwa kinds,

Section 8: The Drug Collecting Season and Produce of the Several Varieties

The collection of drug was begun on the 24th of January and continued until the 24th of March, with the local and Malwa races; while the European sorts, which are always much later than the others, and lanced this season for the first time on the 15th March, continued to yield until the 10th of April. The season, though upon the whole genial for vegetation generally, was anything but favorable to the maturation of the opium juices. To perfect these a large amount of sunlight is indispensable, to fix in sufficient quantity the drug's basic element - carbon.

A really dry atmosphere is also of paramount importance but indeed this is a necessary factor of the preceding as of course with a moist atmosphere the sun's rays are largely intercepted. The mere question of temperature, it would appear, is not at all one of primary importance as under a considerable range of temperature, given only the aforestated conditions, drug of an excellent quality may be produced. It may be as well to state that I refer to the drug for officinal, or if I may be permitted economic use — as with the Chinese for example — and not by any means to the purely medical article. Indeed from the comparison of the chemical analyses of opium produced under a variety of climatic conditions, I am strongly of opinion that temperature has an important influence on the chemical composition of the drug, i.e. in so far as regards two of its most important components, viz. morphine and narceine. I am thus disposed to believe that, within the range of temperature under which the plant will grow and thrive, the lower is favorable to a high proportionate development of morphine, the higher to narcotine as being the more highly carbonised constituent. Anyhow, as I have stated, observations and experience show that cloudy and moist weather are highly unfavorable to the maturation of the opium juices, as shown by the increase of that peculiar educt, called Pussewah. The weather, then, as I have attempted to show, has a paramount influence on the quality of the drug produce of the opium poppy, but it is no less an important agent as affecting the actual quantity of produce. I have attempted to explain the effects of weather conditions on drug exudation in my manual, and subsequent observations fully confirm the explanations there suggested. In the plates accompanying my report for 1873-74 I have illustrated the opium secretive system of the poppy, and those peculiar vessels associated with it, which, under certain atmospheric conditions, promote or repress more or less the exudation of the juices. This I have attempted to show is wholly dependent on the degree of atmospheric pressure; high barometric pressure promoting, and the obverse repressing, the exudation of drug. For the mechanism of the action, I may refer the reader to the report and manual previously alluded to. Thus, simply by careful observations of a carefully tested barometer on Fortiu's principle — which is considered the most reliable — from 2 P.M. to 6 p.m. (during the earlier periods of which the lancing operation is performed, and the exudation of juice mainly finished;, an approximate estimate may be very correctly made of the drug produce for the following morning. The degree of barometric pressure in the morning is immaterial, in so far as regards the actual exudation of juice, though then a rather lower barometric pressure is desirable, especially with a westerly wind, as facilitating the collection of drug from the capsule. It will be easily understood from the above explanation how largely the drug exudation may be affected from day to day by changes of wind, etc, after midday. Thus, with a prevailing east wind (always as it is here more or less moist) the actual drug exudations will be small, though rapidly assuming a bulky look by the absorption of atmospheric moisture. This is of course due, or, as I should perhaps say, largely so, to the temperature of the plant being then— during the day— lower than the atmosphere. On the other hand in the morning, even with a still prevailing east wind, the plant's temperature is higher than the atmosphere; so that instead of contracting moisture it really gives it off, and thus we have the phenomenon of the east wind, as the natives say, eating up tie opium. Of course it but withdraws in part the previously absorbed atmospheric moisture.

I may here take the opportunity of pointing out an important distinction between opium gathered in a moist or dry, and merely a dewy or foggy morning, and that of a normally moist season. In the former instance we have a drug diminished more or less in quantity, but no way inferior in quality, further than as containing a high percentage of moisture. This, however, readily drains off and when absorbed leaves only a solid, not Pussewah, residue. On the other hand, in a really moist season, as the last for example, the drug abounds more or less in the Pussewah educt, as also in hygroscopic moisture, which is most difficult to extract or evaporate, unless recourse be taken to a sand-bath or such like mode of artificially driving off the moisture. With all this, however, we have still left in considerable quantity the Pussewah liquid, which I now think is simply the normal juice exuding in a crude or immature state.

As regards this point I can unfortunately too clearly illustrate the direct influence of season on the opium-poppy, as related to the production of Pussewah in the drug. Thus, with a normally dry season in 1875«76 1 had in this garden from 10.5 maunds of opium only 7 chittacks of Pussewah, whereas during the last season from 8.25 maunds only I had no less than 21 seers. Thus under the same soil conditions we have the clearest evidence as to the effects of a dry and a moist season on the quantity of Pussewah exudings.

The actual rainfall, as we have seen, for the two months February and March was 1.82 inches only. This, I believe, is about 1.25 inches above the usual average for those months. The mere rainfall, however, which occurred on a few days only is a much less important indicator from one point of view than the hygrometer, by which we learn that during February, with several mornings indicating saturation, the monthly average difference was only 1.77, the maximum average at S p.m. 11.64; again in March, with a few mornings indicating saturation, the average difference was 2.64, the maximum at 8 p.m. 14.57. This, again, is very considerably above the usual average of atmospheric moisture, and of course largely explains the comparatively large percentage of Pussewah yielded by this season's opium. Then, again, we have to note the average atmospheric pressure for the month, which— as I insist — is a most important factor, as controlling and regulating the exudation of the opium juices — a high barometer giving rise to more copious exudations than a low barometer and this quite irrespective of their quality or consistence. In a preceding section

I have given the mean average readings of four daily observations for the opium months, February and March; and now, with the exception of giving the monthly minimum and maximum of each observation, I will only add the mean average of the three daily post-meridian observations, as alone affecting the exudation of drug from the capsule — first for February, The barometrical readings, as previously stated, were taken at 2 pm., 4 pm, and 6 pm. Now the mean pressure from these three daily observations was 29.918 the attached thermometer being 65.23.

The maximum and minimum of each observation, with temperature of the attached thermometer, were as follows:

	First	Second	Third
Maximum	62.8 – 30.094	63.3 – 30.038	62.3 – 30.052
Minimum	63.4 – 29.764	63.7 – 29.752	63.5 – 29.752

Again, in March, the mean average of the three daily observations was 29.797 at a mean temperature of 78.13 by the attached thermometer. The maximum and minimum of these were as follows:

	First	Second	Third
Maximum	80.0 – 29.942	75.0 – 29.916	74.0 – 29.902
Minimum	82.0 – 29.712	82.5 – 29.626	79.3 – 29.712

The barometric observations are thus concordant with those of the hygrometer, the one indicating a low average pressure of the atmosphere, the other an unusually high degree of atmospheric moisture- conditions, I need scarcely now add, alike unfavorable to the copious exudation or the complete maturation of the opium juices. This is shown by the fact that the mean average produce of the plant in the gardens here scarcely exceeds that of last year (as limited to the local varieties which disappointed me, as all had been raised from the seed- produce of the most highly productive capsules), whereas as regards Pussewa, the proportion, as I have shown, is no less than 20 to 1, which of course indicates a very large loss of matured drug.

I will now proceed to give a statement of the relative productiveness of each of the varieties separately. First, for Deegah:

(A) Deegah Gardens: their Produce.

1. Tegleah variety. I had in all under this variety 5 beeghas 2 cottahs, the opium outturn of which was 47 seers, i.e, 9 seers 3.25 chittacks per beegha. This is a favorite variety with many of the cultivators, though far less generally grown than it deserves; as for early cropping it is certainly one of the most productive sorts which I have had any experience with, plots of the first sown crop yielding 10.5 seers per beegha, whereas late sowings - and this of the same quality or sample of seed - did not exceed 5 seers. Moreover, 3 beeghas of the above were sown by the 6th of October, and were thus much injured by the subsequent heavy rains immediately following. But for this I should certainly have had a much higher outturn from the first sown crop. As it stands, however, the average is certainly good for the season.

The total weight of sun-dried stalks, excluding capsules and seeds, was 1,210 seers. To ascertain the number of plants per beegha I selected a bundle of average plants weighing off and counting the number in 10 seers of each. 1 thus got an average of 1,020 plants per 10 seers, which of course is equal to about 24,220 plants per beegha only. This was a very low average of plants indeed, and was partly owing to the ultimate failure of many of the young plants exposed to the October rains, and partly, as I have already explained, to over thinning of the latter. 1 have only this season ascertained that the plants raised from my most carefully selected seeds are but little disposed to give off lateral shoots, which I consider an advantage. I shall therefore endeavor to allow fully twice the number of plants in future, or at least have them on an average at distances of nine by ten inches, which gives about 43,560 plants per beegha.

2. Sufaid-danthi, var. This is perhaps one of the most generally cultivated of the several varieties grown in the agencies, though as a rule less productive than the Teyleah variety for early cropping. It, however, is far superior to it for late cropping, and for this reason perhaps it is more generally grown by the Assamese, as a majority of them, from the lateness of their rainy season's crop, are unable to get their lands prepared for early crops of poppy. It is thus probably that it is the more general favorite. Of this variety I had 13 cottahs only sown with very carefully selected seed. The weight of the sun-dried plant there from, excluding capsules and seeds, was 156 seers, with an average plant of 1,016 per 10 seers, which, as in the preceding experimental plot, gives about 24,220 per beegha. The plants were, however, generally more vigorous than that lot, as is shown by the relative number in the weighed bundle. The

drug-produce of this variety was 6 seers 4.5 chittacks, which is about equal to 9 seers 10.5 chittacks per beegha. This plot had an application of lime prior to the sowing of the seed, and subsequently the young plants were top-dressed with shorah and nonimattee. The latter had a striking effect on the crop, greatly increasing the vigor of the plants and imparting a deeper green to the foliage,

3. Kutila, var. — I have specially recommended this variety in previous reports, as better than any of those ordinarily cultivated for withstanding hail-storms and high winds. This it does from its much reduced and narrowly segmented foliage of thick and dense texture. It also better than any of the other commonly cultivated sorts, resists those blights to which all are more or less subject. I know not why this excellent variety is not more generally cultivated. My experimental plot comprised exactly two beeghas. The total weight of sun-dried plant was 485 seers, the weighed average sample of 10 seers containing 1,035 plants, which is equal to about 25,100 plants per beegha. This was a very fair average, but unfortunately few of the plants bore more than two capsules, and a majority of them bore only one. I might thus have grown with advantage fully twice the number of plants, and I doubt not would thus have doubled the opium return. The actual drug return of these two beeghas was 18 seers 11 chittacks, i.e. 9 seers 5.5 chittacks per beegha.

I have now in small quantity seeds of a new race of this variety, which promises to be a more copious drug-producer than its parent.

4. Choura-kutila - this is also an excellent variety, though less grown than any of those noticed above. It differs chiefly from the last in having thinner and less narrowly and deeply cut foliage. It differs, in so far as my experience goes, from that variety also in preferring heavier soils. For example, under the same conditions of moisture, the kutila, var., will succeed in a sandy loam, while the other — Choura-kutila requires a strong and retentive clayey loam. Requiring more moisture than the other variety, it has last season suffered less from the excess which we had, and accordingly somewhat exceeds it in fertility, as I will now show. — Well, I had in all 2 beeghas 15 cottahs under this variety. The total weight of plant was 580 seers, averaging 1,028 plants per 10 seers. This affords us an average of about 21,680 plants per beegha. It should be observed that though there were a considerably smaller number of plants in this plot than in the preceding, it took the eye more favorably, the plants being taller and more vigorous, and the foliage more fully developed. The opium produce of this variety was 28 seers 9 chittacks, which of course is equal to 10 seers 6 chittacks per beegha. I have now in small quantity seed of a very promising, early-cropping race of the above variety.

5. Kaladaniki - This is an excellent and favorite variety, and perhaps more generally cultivated than either of the two last named. It is well marked by the peculiar bluish-black color acquired by the flower-stalk soon after the fall of the flower. This is a less robust variety than any of the preceding. It is, however, a

copious drug-producer, and the capsules attaining as a rule the drug-yielding stage very uniformly, it has a less protracted season than any of the other varieties known to me. This, I need scarcely remark, is a very desirable quality. In so far as my experience goes, however, it gives better returns as an early than a late cropper. My experimental plot of this variety comprised 3 beeghas, the total weight of sun-dried plants on which was 818 seers, affording an average number of 1,125 plants per 10 seers, which is equal to about 27,540 per beegha. The return of opium was in all 29 fleers 1 chittack, or 9 seers 11 chittacks per beegha. Though there was in this plot a larger number of plants per beegha than in any of the others, it by no means appeared so to the eye, the habit of the plant being altogether more slender and compact. As thus requiring considerably less space than the others, it might be grown with advantage at a distance of 9 by 9 inches, that is to say 48,400 plants per beegha.

6. Subza Kaladanthiy - This is a very distinct new race of the preceding variety, of which a single specimen was picked out of a plot in the fields here three years ago. It is a very productive sort, but this last season, as I believe, from the unusual moisture, though the lands had a fair manurial application, the plant did not acquire its usual vigor, and yielded considerably less than its ordinary average of drug. I had 4 beeghas 12 cottahs under this variety; but as one of the plots was much later in season than the others, and considerably lees productive, I will give the results separately. Thus, in the one series I had 8 beeghas 12 cottahs of plant, the sun dried stalks of which weighed 780 seers, the bundle of seers contained 1,860 plants. The average number of plants per beegha was thus 29,460. This is of course a fair amount of plant, but all were slender and dwarf; the stalks as a rule simple, and thus producing but a single capsule. The return of drug was 30 seers 3 chittacks, i.e. on an average 8 seers 6 chittacks per beegha. The other plot of one beegha was much later in season than the preceding, the first collection of opium having been made on the 1st of March, whereas the others came in season from the 3rd to the 10th of February. The late plant was more spare and dwarf than the early sown, and only afforded eight collections of drug. The general results are as follow: The weight of sun-dried stalks was 190 seers only, whereas the number of average plants in a bundle of 10 seers was 1,580, which is equal to about 30,000 per beegha. It is to be observed, however, that the plants were altogether stunted, nearly all with short simple stalks from 16 to 18 inches high, the capsules small and scant of drug. The total return in opium was only 5 seers.

This variety, more than any other I am acquainted with, is alike impatient to heat and excess of moisture in the atmosphere or the soil. I can, however, favorably recommend it for an early crop on light well-drained soil. When coming in late in the season, say March, the sun-heat is too great for it; the capsules become shriveled and discolored, drying up prematurely and yielding little drug. The parent of this, the well-known kaladanthi, though less impatient than the latter to high temperatures, is nevertheless considerably more highly productive as an early than a late cropper.

Indeed I may as well introduce here the conclusions I have arrived at from careful observations of the plant in the field for several successive seasons - as to a distinguishing and easily recognized character of these varieties specially suited for early cropping. Well, the many varieties of the opium-poppy are, as we all know, easily separable into two well-marked races by the color, or polish and texture of the capsule, the one being distinguished by capsules of an opaque green in deeper or paler shades: this comprises the sabza-dherri varieties of the Assamese. The other has glaucous capsules, or more or less densely coated with an opaque white powder: this is the sufaid-dherri sorts of the Assamese. Now, I find that while the latter, or sufatd-dherri race, may be indifferently used for late or early cropping the former, or sabza-dherri race, is peculiarly suited for early cropping ; and though, with the exception perhaps of the kaladanthi variety, the later crops may not be wanting in vegetative vigor, nevertheless they will be found to yield much less drug. Under a March sun the milk system of this sabza'dherri race is very rapidly exhausted and scarcely a moiety of their normal drug- produces extractable. I am now fully convinced of the special adaptability of this race for early sowing, and shall thus accordingly regulate any of my future experiments with it. The special peculiarities of the two races is probably wholly due to difference in polish and texture of the capsule— that with the white powdery coating better resisting evaporative action in a high temperature and a dry atmosphere than the smooth and polished surface of the other.

7. Monaria - My selected and improved race of this variety is a copious drug- producer, but more than others requiring a well-manured soil, and that of the strong clay loam sort. In light sandy soils it is less productive; the capsules are also smaller, of an ovate-oblong shape, and then scarcely distinguishable from the common sufaid-dherri variety. The area under cultivation with this variety was one beegha. The weight of sun-dried stalk 245 seers; a bundle of average plant of 10 seers containing 950 plants, which is equal to about 28,075 per beegha. As indicated by the number of average plants in a bundle of 10 seers, this will be found to have been somewhat more vigorous than any of the other varieties. It also yielded in crude drug a larger quantity than any of the others, but unfortunately, as containing a very large amount of pussewa and hygroscopic moisture, it did not quite reach the maximum standard in pure opium, this being only 9 seers 9 chittacks. With a greater amount of sun-light and a drier atmosphere, for the due maturation of the drug on the one hand and the promotion of its exudation on the other, the net produce in opium would have been very much higher. These remarks are, however, more or less applicable to all the varieties.

8. Dherri-danthi var. This is a new race, given off by the common sufaid-dherri, and the cultivation of which I have from year to year increased, as being much less subject to the common poppy blight than any of the old varieties. Unfortunately it has always proved a very scant drug producer. This defect I hoped, and indeed still do hope, to obviate by the careful selection of seeds from the most copious drug-producing capsules only ; and this I am the more encouraged to do as affording a superior medical opium— containing a higher percentage of morphine. This is an important property aside from the

comparative blight immunity. Moreover last season, 1875-76, it considerably increased its fertility and gave me an average of 5 seers 10.5 chittacks per beegha of very fine opium. I this season therefore extended its cultivation, and in the Deegah gardens alone I had 84 beeghas under it. It failed signally, as the following results will show, and I now strongly suspect that it is one of those which require not only a light and dry soil, but also a considerable degree of atmospheric dryness for anything like successful cultivation. Its cultivation should thus be continued in a very small scale, and this only with a view to its selective improvement in the desiderated qualities noticed above.

In the 3.5 beeghas, I had in all 675 seers of sun-dried stalks, and 1,150 average plants per bundle of 10 seers, which is equal to about 22,180 per beegha. The net produce in opium was 11 seers 2.5 chittacks, that is, the low average of 3 seers 3 chittacks per beegha. The results are very disappointing as compared with those of the previous season. Its several good properties, however, recommend it as a subject well worthy of experiments on a small scale, and this of course with a view to its selective improvement.

9. Variegated poppy. This is another new race of the sufaid-dherri variety, which is but little liable to blight affections. This comparative exemption from blight is, I believe, as explained in previous reports, attributable to the more highly oxygenised state of the tissues generally than that of the unvariegated or normal forms. This, I think, is well shown by the fact that the white portions of the leaf, as a rule, resist the invasions of the blight fungus, and this of course as being the most highly oxygenised parts. It, like the preceding, however, has the bad quality of being a very scant drug-producer. It differs from the latter, however, in its opium containing morphine and narcotine in nearly equal quantities, and also in giving less in total alkaloids by 4.94 per cent, than that variety. The general results of my experiments with this variety during the past season are as follows. The area under cultivation was 12 cottahs: the plant healthy and vigorous, forming quite a full and uniform crop. The capsules were also well developed, but from their poorly developed milk-system they scarcely gave on an average two drug incisions each, and the total produce in opium was only 1 seer 12 chittacks; that is, 2 seers 14.5 chittacks per beegha. I have only retained for next season's experiments, with this variety, a small quantity of seed from the most copious drug-producing capsules. Of course its comparative immunity from blight is a highly important quality, and it is quite possible that by experiment and selection it may yet give rise to a race which, while retaining the former quality, has also acquired that of being a copious drug-producer.

10» Sufaid'danthi Monaria. This is an excellent mongrel variety raised by intercrossing the beading varieties. It is of extremely vigorous habit, and produces large and uniform capsules of a roundish-oblong shape. In the season of 1875-76 I made no attempt to select the seedy haying in all but two seers, which this season I sowed on 12 cottahs. It germinated well, produced a vigorous and uniform crop: the total weight of sun-dried plant being 210 seers, of which a bundle of 10 seers contained 840 average sized plants, which is equal to about 29,400 per beegha. The net produce in opium was six seers; that is, ten seers per beegha. The approaching season will, I hope, afford me a very much higher return, as I have now a small quantity of seed selected from the largest and most copious drug-producing capsules.

11. Monaria Teyleah, — This is also a mongrel race, originating from an intercross of the two varieties named. It promises to be a copious drug-producer. It resembles its female parent monaria in general habit and form of capsule, while the polish and texture of the latter is quite the teyleah type, and of a deep opaque green. I had for the past season a sufficiency of seed for 8 cottahs only. The sun-dried stalks weighed 130 seers, and a bundle of 10 seers contained 915 average plants, which is equal to about 29,780 per beegha. The net return in opium of this plant was 3 seers 13.5 chittacks; that is to say, 9 seers 9.5 chittacks per beegha. This and the preceding variety are thus likely to prove valuable additions to the opium grower.

B. Hill Poppy. This is a variety referred to in the Agent's summary of last season's (1875-76) experiments with selected seeds from this garden in the Benares Agency. Mr. Luard, who is the introducer of this variety, states that the seed was said to be procured from some village considerably to the north of Simla. From its succeeding so well, however, in the plains of India on its first introduction, there is clearly some mistake as to its origin. Hill poppies, and especially those from such high elevations, do not readily habituate themselves to culture in the plains.

The Agent of Benares sent me a parcel of seed of this variety, which enabled me to sow up a plot of 12 cottahs. The seed was of excellent quality, germinating freely and rapidly. The plant also grew up and flowered simultaneously with the other local sorts. In habit it is not at all distinguishable from the common sufaid-dherri variety of the natives, but again pretty fairly distinguished from it by the more oblong capsule: this, however, being glaucous in both. One feature which I particularly observed in the lancing of this plant was that the capsules, though of full size, firm and plump, gave remarkably little opium to the first and second incisions. To the third and subsequent, including the fifth, the exudations were fairly copious. Few of them, however, afforded more than six incisions, the average four only. The general results were as follow: The total weight of sun-dried stalks was 235 seers, the bundle of 10 seers containing 785 average plants, which is equal to about 28,780 per beegha. The plot was very uniformly filled with a vigorous plant. The opium-collecting season extended from the 3rd of February to the 5th March. The net produce of opium was 4 seers 2 chittacks, the average per beegha being thus 6 seers 14 chittacks. This is of course below the average of all the old varieties cultivated in the gardens here.

6. In all the above experiments the ridge mode of culture was adopted. I now pass on to those under the native mode of plane surface culture. As I have previously stated, I had in all four beeghas only under the latter system. Previous to sowing up, this had a liberal application of decayed poppy trash, lime, and

charcoal. The kinds and quality of the seeds used were as follow: Two beeghas were sown up with seeds retained on a sieve with meshes 1/22nd of an inch on the side of the square. Two varieties were used, viz. teyleah and sabza kaladanthi. The third beegha was sown with small-sized seeds of the former variety, those only which passed a sieve of 1/27th of an inch on the side of the square. The fourth was sown with seeds of the sufaid-danthi, and the successive produce for five seasons of untapped capsules. The results were as follows:

A. First, for the two beeghas of teyleah and kaladanthi with the large sized-seeds. A few days after the sowing of the seeds we had a shower of rain, which laid on somewhat consolidated the surface soil, which formed a thin firm crust in drying, sufficient to impede germination, so that the young germs were mainly confined to the lines of cracks formed by the shrinkage of the soil. This, however, would have afforded a far from full or uniform crop, so that partial re-sowings had to be made after the first irrigation of the young plants. This gave rise to a fairly uniform crop. As compared with the ridged crops, sown at the same time, the growth especially in the earlier stages was alike less vigorous and rapid, and the former - the ridged crop - attained the drug-yielding stage eight days before the latter. The total weight of sun-dried stalks on the two beeghas was 412 seers, a bundle of 10 seers containing 1,820; that is to say, 27,985 per beegha. This, in so far as regards number, is very fair; but, as in all the plants from selected seed, a great majority bore but a single terminal capsule, and of the others few exceeded two or three. All my selected seed crops have thus more or less suffered from overt binning the young plant. I do not doubt the district experiments with my selected seeds have been similarly vitiated, as the officers in charge would naturally have the young plants thinned out to the usual distance. I had not at all anticipated that the mode of selection practiced would have thus altered the general habit of the plant. The net produce of opium from the two beeghas was 14 seers 3 chittacks this being produced in nearly equal proportions by the two varieties.

B. Teyleah; seeds passed by a 1/27th inch mesh. In the preceding experiment seeds retained by a 1/27th of an inch sieve were used; in the present case those only which passed through the 1/27th of an inch sieve were used. As regards germination, the results in both were very similar, partial re-sowing being necessary to secure anything like a uniform crop.

Now, as regards the vigor and habit of the plant comparatively with that raised from the larger sized seeds, the former was easily distinguished as being alike of sparer habit and lower growth. This is dearly shown by the following general results on comparison with those from the larger sized seeds. Thus the total weight of sun-dried stalks was 191 seers, of which a handle of 10 seers counted 1,580 average plants; that is to say, 30,178 per beegha. With the smaller sized plant, however, and the largely increased number, they fell far short in the relative drug produce: this being only 4 seers 14 chittacks, whereas in the larger-sized seed crop the return was 7 seers 1.5 chittacks. Plainly, therefore, the small sized seeds afford a very considerably poorer crop of opium plants than those of larger size. These results, I will only add here, is quite concordant with those of previous years' experiments.

D. Seeds from untapped capsules.

The results of this are of considerable interest, practically and theoretically ; it having, on the one hand, been held that the seeds produced by capsules from which the opium juices had not been extracted gave rise to a more copious drug.- producing progeny than those from which it had been taken ; and again, on the other hand, that by the continued extraction of this juice the plant would soon reach the zero of reproduction, and of course die off, or, as generally expressed, 'go to the wall'. Both of these views are alike incorrect, as I find that non-extraction of drug from the capsules tends to diminish instead of increasing the secretion of drug in the progeny. Again, as regards the other assumption, viz. that the milky juice of the opium poppy, as that of all similarly characterized plants, is a highly elaborated and highly organized fluid, and really of vital importance in the economy of the plant. This is clearly a mistaken notion, and is well disproved by the continued vigor of the opium poppy after having been from generation to generation utterly depleted of its milk juice for, I may say, centuries past; nevertheless the poppy growing in any well-manured field now is not a whit less vigorous, and certainly quite as copious a drug-producer as any of its progenitors.

Seeing, then, that the milk/juice does not in any apparent way contribute to the functions of nutrition or reproduction, it may well be asked what purpose is it really subservient to in the plant's economy? I could myself have offered no explanation to this question, but it so happens that Mr. Darwin in a late letter gives me the key. He somewhat struck with my observation as to the inutility of the milk-juice in the functions of nutrition or reproduction, and having then read, which I had not, Mr. Kerner's admirable paper "On The Means Of Protecting Flowers From Unwelcome Visitors" very naturally suggested to me that the function of the milk-juice may very probably be of a protective nature. As regards the poppy, I believe he is quite right; and I do not doubt that this will be found to hold in all other milk-juiced plants. However, I have here to do with the opium poppy only. Now, as illustrating the protective influence of the milk-juice in it, I have observed that the caterpillars of one species of noctua cause great damage to the young plant, while the milk-juice is quite or almost bland - so bland indeed that the leaves form an excellent substitute for lettuce. The advanced plant is free from its attack, as is shown by the fact that in partially sown fields, while the older plants are exempt, the younger are alone infested. Again, another caterpillar of the same genus eats its way into the capsule and greedily devours the seeds. This it does, however, only after the milk-juice has been extracted from the capsule. Thus, under cultivation we have in the above cases two capital illustrations of the protective influence of the milk -juice in the poppy. I will not dwell further on this here, however, but pass on at once to the results of my experiment with the seeds from untapped capsules.

Well, the seeds forming the subjects of this experiment were collected by myself last season from untapped capsules, as had those producing them for four previous generations. They thus give rise to a fifth generation of plants from which the opium-juices have not been extracted. Now, this seed differed in no way, either as regards size or specific gravity, from that ordinarily found in the Assamese' field. The general results are as follow:

One beegha of land under experiment gave a total weight in sun-dried stalk of 225 seers, of which a bundle of 10 seers contained 1,125 average sized plants; that is equal to 28,562 plants per beegha. As compared with the plant on the adjoining plot, they were more freely branched, so that they bore a considerably higher number of capsules, and thus relatively ought to have afforded a more copious supply of drug. The net produce, however, in opium was only three seers, whereas, as above shown, the produce of selected seed from regularly drug-extracted capsules gave under the same soil conditions, etc., 7 seers 11 chittacks.

We have thus, I think, the clearest evidence that the non-extraction of the milky juice from the opium poppy tends to lessen the secretion in the progeny, thus deteriorating the plant as an opium-yielder.

E. The Malwa variety of the opium poppy.

This last season, as I have already remarked, proved altogether unsuited to all the Malwa race of poppy. I was greatly disappointed in this result, as last year, 1875-76, very fair returns of opium, and the apparent perfect acclimatization of the plant, induced me to sow several large plots of land with seeds of the different varieties in various parts of the garden. All were alike unsuccessful, and gave really miserable returns. My only object in increasing the cultivation of these varieties here was the hope of getting the white-flowered races thoroughly adapted to soil and climate, and thus to gradually supplant some of the local sorts, which certainly, from a medical point of view, produce an inferior drug. This season's results are, however, vexations and utterly discouraging.

I had in all at Deegah 6 beeghas 14 cottahs under the varieties of Malwa poppy. Of this 4 beeghas 10 cottahs were sown on the 6th and 7th of October, and were thus subjected to the more or less heavy showers which fell daily from the latter date to the 18th instant. As all the surface, however, had been ridged, the seeds germinated freely; and there was no occasion for re-sowing, as after the rains there was an abundance of young plants. As they attained their fourth and fifth leaves, all had a pale, sickly, green color, and quite an unhealthy look. I then gave them a liberal top-dressing with nonimaitee. This stimulated them some- what, and about twelve days later I top-dressed them again with a mixture of nonimattee and lime. They were much benefited by this. Early in January, however, plants here and there — miserable little plants not over three inches in height — burst into flower. Fearing that all might thus prematurely flower, I gave them for the third time an application of nonimattee. This, however, at best had but a very temporary effect, as by the middle of January all had thus prematurely flowered; scarcely a single plant exceeding eighteen inches in height, the majority indeed not twelve inches. All had simple stalks, terminating in a miserable little capsule, which it would have simply been labor lost to have lanced. I, however, had all the larger sized capsules from time to time lanced, and even these ill repaid the labor; the net produce of opium from the whole of the 4.5 beeghas being only 2 seers 9.5 chittacks — that is to say, about 9.25 chittacks per beegha, a miserable return indeed for labor and other expenses.

I regret to say that the later sown plant did very little better. This comprised an area of 2 beeghas 4 cottahs, and was sown from the 18th to the 20th of October. The ridged system was adopted with all, the germination free and rapid. Escaping, as they did, the October rains, which had, as I then supposed, been the main cause of the first crop, they presented an altogether healthier appearance, though far from attaining at any stage the vigor of the preceding season's crop. They might thus indeed have given a fair return of drug but for the heavy showers of rain on the 12th and 13th of January, partly accompanied and succeeded by strong gusts of wind from the north-east, which simply prostrated the whole plant. The first collection of opium was made on the 20th of February, the last on the 22nd of March. The net return of all in opium was 3 seers 13.5 chittacks, which is to say about 1 seer 9.5 chittacks per beegha. Thus the general average for the 6 beeghas 14 cottahs devoted to the Malwa poppies was only 15.25 chittacks per beegha.

The maximum average of the above races in Deegah last year (1875-76) was 8 seers 12 chittacks per beegha, and as I had been especially careful in the selection of seed for the past season's experiment I certainly anticipated an average return of at least 10 seers per beegha. Their failure, I repeat, can only be attributed to the unusual moistness of the season. The pure Malwa poppies, after five seasons' cultivation in Behar, being thus liable to failures in more than an averagely moist season, their cultivation may be practically and fiscally abandoned. On a very small scale, however, I would propose to continue experiments with a few of the most promising of the mongrel races, which I have raised by the intercrossing of the Malwa with the local race.

F. The European varieties of the opium poppy

In compliance with a previous requisition, I received from the Board a parcel of seeds directly imported from Europe, of the Turkey and Spanish opium poppy, with two varieties, each of Italian and French origin. These reached me about the end of October 1875. The seeds generally germinated well, and the plant was singularly vigorous and robust. The Italian and Turkey gave very fair returns of excellent opium;

the Spanish and French were but poorly productive, though both considerably more so than were any of the Malwa race when first introduced into Behar. They also differed from the latter in the soil and climate, being well-suited to their mere growth, as all were of a taller habit, with thicker stalks and larger foliage than any of the local varieties. There was thus, both as regards vegetation and drug produce, every reason to anticipate their becoming a valuable addition to the local race. I thus utilized all the seed return of that season during the past, and had in all, in the Deegah gardens, above 4 beeghas 10 cottahs of European poppy. The several plots of the different varieties were nearly all sown between the 18th and 24th of October. Two only of the varieties failed, or nearly so, viz. one of French and one of Italian origin. These plots were subsequently sown with seeds of the Turkey poppy.

The seeds, with the exception, of course, of the two varieties noted, germinated very freely, and in about the same period as those of the local varieties. The young plant, as compared with that of the preceding season, was less impatient to the usual low temperatures of December and the first half of January, though still of much more tardy growth than any of local origin. It made thus, upon the whole, but little progress until the middle of January, when it began to give out a series of large root leaves. To any one, however, who had seen those of the previous season, it was apparent that they were of a smaller size and paler color, the plant being thus altogether less vigorous and healthy. In the early part of February the flower-stalk in a few began to show, but it was near the middle of the month before it was at all general. The first flowers began to expand about the end of February, were general by the 6th of March, and afforded a set of capsules for a first collection of drug on the 16th of March.

Thus, though sown about the same time as many of the local sorts, they only began to yield opium when these had been depleted. This is of course a bad characteristic of the European race, though probably it may be eliminated in the process of acclimatization. From the 16th of March to the 9ih of April we had more or less regular collections of drug. Before this, how- ever, by much the larger proportion of plant had been dried up prematurely with dry westerly winds and the high temperature.

There is another evil attending their lateness in flowering, and which I only detected during the past season. First, I may explain that on the first flowering of the several varieties in this garden all, with one exception, had white flowers, that red. I having no suspicion of intercrossing being affected, from the purity of all the local varieties from season to season when grown alongside of each other, was not a little surprised, when the several varieties began to open, to find them presenting a variety of shades of color between white and red. Indeed, in some of the plots the latter color and its shades were more common than the white. I was quite at a loss to explain this. Winds and, insects are the main agents in the natural fertilization of plants. Now, of course, late and early crops are alike exposed to pollen—wafting winds, and as regards insects I had often remarked the poverty of our poppy fields in flower-haunting insects during the day and of course the visits of moths, &g., during the night were debarred by the complete closure of the flowers shortly after sunset.

By a little observation, however, this season, I had an early explanation of the mystery. Amongst the earlier flowers even I observed a few specimens of two species of small bees flying from flower to flower collecting pollen. Of course I had then no longer doubt as to the fertilizing agent and the cause of my present season's mongrel crops. Later on both species of bees so abounded that scarcely a grain of pollen could be found an hour or so after the expansion of the flower. I have indeed counted late in the season, when the flowers were somewhat scarce, from ten to eighteen of these little bees in a single flower ; all, strangely enough, though of two quite distinct species, working happily and diligently without intrusion on one another specifically or individually, the most perfect mutuality prevailing. The result of this prodigence of pollen by these insects is that fertilization was most imperfect, and the capsules yielded scarcely any seed; the whole produce of the several varieties being only 13 seers.

Making due allowance for the lateness of the crop, I should at least have had 260 seers. This late cropping tendency of the European varieties is a serious drawback to their introduction. However, as previously observed, this will doubtless give way in the course of a few seasons' culture if care is only taken to select seeds from the earliest flowering plants. They are anyhow well worth the experiment, from the present high vigor of the plant and the very superior quantity of opium, as a purely official article.

I have now only to add that as the varieties individually really produced such a small quantity of drug, I did not think it worth separate storage. The net produce in opium of the four and a half beeghas was only three seers 10 chittacks, that is to say, about 12.75 chittacks per beegha. This is a great falling off as compared with last season's returns. The returns of the Malwa and European varieties have thus been alike vexatiously low and discouraging.

G. The opium produce of the Meetapore Garden

As previously stated, this garden comprises an area of 12 beeghas 18 cottahs. During the past season a few plots in the garden had an application of refuse matters from the jail, which is regularly thrown out in a waste corner of the lands under my charge. This is very serviceable. The only additional manure used last season was nonimattee which was applied from time to time in the way of a top-dressing to the plant at different stages. In all I thus used of the latter 20 cart-loads of from 16 to 20 maunds each.

In a previous section, on the general appearance of the crop in the season of vegetation. I have remarked that none of the plant in the gardens here attained anything like the vigor of that of the previous season. This I can only attribute to the water logging of the soil after portions had been sown, and immediately previous to the completion of the whole. The more retentive nature of the soil in this garden, relatively to that generally characteristic of Deegah, exaggerated the evil, and the result was that even with my best selected seeds the average return of opium fell rather below that of Deegah. In previous seasons it has invariably afforded the higher average. Deegah, however, has always had this advantage, that while the Meetapore lands have been long under cultivation and thoroughly well pulverized those of the former are only lately broken up, and thus less suited to the requirements of the poppy. The four seasons of tillage which they have now had has improved them greatly and from the repeated tilling they are undergoing this season at every favorable opportunity of weather I hope to have them in excellent condition for next season's crop.

The collection of opium in the Meetapore garden was more or less regularly continued from the 1st of February to the 23rd of March. I have already remarked on the general unfavorability of the season for the copious production of a high class drug. This was especially felt on the comparatively retentive soil of the Meetapore gardens. It was, moreover, aggravated by occasional falls of rain, which not only caused a direct loss in washing opium from the lanced capsules, but deteriorated and impeded exudations for a few subsequent days.

I will now give a separate statement of the general appearance of the plant as it matured, and the net produce in opium of each variety.

I. Kutila variety.

I had in all five plots of this variety, in different portions of the garden. One plot of these was sown previous to the October rains, the others subsequently, from the 18th to the 23rd instant. Well, though the most productive of all the old varieties in the Meetapore garden in the season of 1875-76, it was with a single exception the least productive in the immediately past season. The plant nowhere acquired its usual vigor; all shooting up to flower prematurely. The total weight of sun-dried plant was considerably less per beegha than that of the same variety in the Deegah gardens. Thus, while at Deegah we had an average of 242 seers per beegha, that of Meetapore was only 195 seers. The details are as follow:

The total weight of sun-dried stalks in the three beeghas was 585 seers, of which one bundle of 10 seers contained 1,215 average plants, which of course is equal to 23,682 per beegha. The average size of the Meetapore plants was considerably under that of Deegah; moreover, nearly all of them had simple stalks, and of course but one capsule. The net produce in opium was 27 seers 8 chittacks, which is equal to 9 seers 2.5 chittacks per beegha.

2. Monaria variety

The general condition of this excellent variety was upon the whole good. Less than any of the others did it seem to suffer from the excess of soil-moisture, as it was certainly the heaviest plant in the gardens; though, again, more than any of the varieties did the drug abound in Pussewah, otherwise the net produce in opium would have been considerably higher. The general results are as follows. The area under cultivation was 1.5 beeghas; the total weight of sun-dried stalks 380 seers, of which a bundle of 10 seers contained 925 average plants, that is to say 23,432 per beegha. This was of course a fairly full crop in so far as regards mere number; but unfortunately the individual plants rarely bore more than two or three capsules, so that at least one-third more plants might have been added with advantage. The produce in opium was in all 16 seers 7 chittacks, that is to say 10 seers 15 chittacks per beegha. Thus, giving due allowance for the really unfavorable season and the great loss in Pussewah and hygroscopic moisture, this was a very fair return.

8. Subza- Kaladanthi.

This new variety gave a somewhat higher return of drug in the Meetapore garden than at Deegah. This, however, I believe was wholly due to its forming an earlier crop, as the average plant was the lighter of the two, as will be seen by a comparison of the following general statement of the weight etc. of stalks of the Meetapore with that of Deegah. The area under cultivation was in all 1.25 beeghas; the total weight of sun- dried stalks 260 seers, of which a bundle of 10 seers contained 1,475 average plants, that is to say 29,500 per beegha. Now, the opium produce was in all 11 seers 11 chittacks; the average return per beegha being thus 9 seers 5.25 chittacks.

This variety, I do not doubt, will prove a most valuable addition to the older sorts of the Assamese. Especially will it be found useful for early cropping. The plant also, as being naturally less robust than the others, does well in a light sandy soil.

4. Kaladanthi variety

This, the parent of the preceding variety, was somewhat the less productive of the two in the Meetapore garden. The plant indeed was somewhat the more vigorous, but the number of plants per beegha was considerably less, and consequently the number of capsules, which of course explains the discrepancy in the relative returns of opium. Thus the weight of sun-dried stalk from the plot of 12 cottahs was 168 seers, of which a bundle of 10 seers contained in average 1,215 plants, which of course gives an average of about 24,020, that is to say 5,480 plants per beegha less than the subza-kaladanthi in the adjoining plots. The net produce in opium was 5 seers 1 chittack, that is to say 8 seers 7 chittacks per beegha.

I would here again remark that it is very desirable that this variety should be more generally cultivated, as being well suited to all the lighter descriptions of soils-— the sandy-loams, or loamy sands— and as having a less protracted opium season than any of the other varieties known to me, while falling no way short in the average returns. These, and especially the latter, are of prime importance in opium produce, as affording high returns of drug in a short season.

5. Teyleah variety.

This variety, though generally the most productive of all the older varieties, gave during the past season the most scanty returns. More than any of them did it suffer from the excess average moisture of soil and atmosphere. I can at least offer no other explanation for the relatively low drug returns. Moreover, the plant did not acquire anything like its usual vigor, the average plant being about three feet in height only, the foliage small and of a pale sickly green — unmistakable evidence of inaptitude to soil or climate. The area under cultivation was 1 beegha 16 cottahs; the total weight of sun-dried stalks from which was only 482 seers, the bundle of 10 seers containing 1,120 average plants, the average per beegha being thus 26,880. The produce in opium was only 9 seers 14 chittacks, that is to say, 5 seers 7.75 chittacks per beegha— an unusually low average indeed for this excellent variety. I should add that it is very probable the circumstance of its being the latest sown of the Meetapore set and consequently the last to attain the drug-yielding stage has something to do with its unusually small return of opium.

6. Monaria-kaladanthi Variety

This is a new and extremely prolific variety, of robust habit, originating in an intercross of the above well-known varieties. It partakes most of the monaria variety in general habit, form, and size of capsules, while clearly enough showing its kaladanthi extraction in the flower-stalks, which, shortly after the fall of the flower, assume the peculiar bluish-black color characteristic of that variety. As the last season was only the second since its origin, I had only a small quantity of seed for trial, and of course no selection was made for that crop. The returns nevertheless, as I will now show, are most satisfactory. I had seed sufficient for a quarter of a beegha only of this variety, which was sown on the 22nd of October, began to flower early in February, the first collection of drug being made on the 19th instant and the last on the 21st March, The total weight of sun-dried stalks from the five cottahs under this variety was 95 seers, of which a bundle, weighing 10 seers, contained 750 average plants, and hence an average per beegah of 28,500. The opium produce of this plot was 3 seers 12.5 chittacks, which is equal to 15 seers 2 chittacks per beegha.

This during the past season has proved the most highly productive of all the varieties cultivated in the gardens under my charge. I have now made a careful selection of seed from the most highly productive capsules, and I do not doubt the next season— if at all favorable to opium produce, which the past certainly was not — will afford us a much higher return.

7. Derhi-danthi variety

This, a variation of the safaid-danthi variety, specially characterized by a comparative immunity from the common blight of the opium poppy (as previously noticed in the report on the Deegah cultivation), had a larger area of land allotted to it than most of the others. Clearly, however, this variety is impatient to any excess of moisture in soil or atmosphere if at all prolonged, as for instance in the past season, which, from beginning to end, so much exceeded the normal average. This hairy-stalked variety, judging comparatively from the results of the past and previous seasons, appears to be peculiarly suited to a light, well-drained soil and a dry rather than a moist atmosphere. To the excess of moisture in both soil and atmosphere I can only attribute its really miserable returns of opium during the past season. The following are the general results. — The area under cultivation was two and a half beeghas; the weight of sun-dried stalks 425 seers, of which a bundle of ten seers contained 1,225 average plants, that is to say 20,820 per beegha. The net produce in opium was four seers one chittack, which gives the miserable return of one seer and ten chittacks per beegha. I need scarcely add that, as in the case of the Deegha experiment with this variety, every body, however, who knows anything of experimental work, will readily admit that there may be, and as a rule are, many failures in obtaining a successful result. This is a case in point, vexatiously disappointing to me, the preceding season's results being full of promise.

8. Variegated Poppy.

The preceding variety, as I have stated, is one of those which is but little liable to be affected by that common blight, of fungus origin, which periodically causes so much damage to the crop. The present variety, even, more than that, obtains this immunity.

This, as I have explained, is wholly due to a simple chemical peculiarity, viz. that its tissues or juices are too highly oxygenated for any rapid or extensive development of that particular parasitic fungus which causes the blight. From season to season I have thus increased the cultivation of this variety, with a view to its improvement as a drug-producer. Hitherto, unfortunately, it has proved one of the most scantily productive in this respect; but of course its comparative immunity from blight is a most valuable quality, and all experience favors the belief that the exaltation of the drug secretions is a mere question of time, experiment, and careful selection. To this end, then, I allotted 1.25 beeghas to this variety in the Meetapore gardens. The plant made favorable progress, though never acquiring anything like the vigor of the Deegah plant. It so happened, however, that the portion of land allotted to it at Meetapore was the lowest, and consequently the wettest of the whole garden. This, no doubt, partly explains the less vigorous habit of the Meetapore plant. The following are the general returns of the crop.

The total weight of sun-dried stalks from the I.25 beeghas was 260 seers, of which a bundle of 10 seers contained 1,120 average plants, thus affording an average of about 22,300 per beegha. The produce in opium was very miserable indeed, being in all 1 seer 13 chittacks only. Thus low though the drug returns of the Deegah plants were, the Meetapore were considerably poorer, the average of the former being 2 seers 14.5 chittacks per beegha, whereas in the latter it was but 1 seer 7 chittacks! I should have previously noticed, however, a difference in the quality of the seeds, those sown at Deegah being much the better, as comprising only such as were retained by a sieve of the 1/27th of an inch mesh, whereas those sown at Meetapore were the passed residue of the above.

9. The Turkey variety.

This variety, as being the only one of which I had seed to spare from the Deegah experiments, with the European sorts, was allotted 15 cottahs in the Meetapore garden. The previous season it was the tallest and most robust of all the varieties; moreover, it was fairly productive in drug, giving an average of three seers four and a half chittacks of excellent opium per beegha. Thus encouraged, I tried it on the above allotment of the Meetapore garden. The seed was sown on the 20th October, and germinated upon the whole feebly, and much more tardily than that of the local sorts. So also its subsequent growth; and moreover in January, after the rainfall on the 12th and 13th instant, I had almost every other day or so a large sized bundle of plants extracted, in a simply rotten state with gangrene. Moist nights with sunny days very soon decimated the crop, and what was left made really no progress. There could be no question as to the prevalence of gangrene being due to the excess of moisture in soil and atmosphere, as also the subsequent arrest of growth in the plant generally. They thus lingered on, rather dying than living, through February and March, when a very small percentage bore flowers. In no single instance, however, did they produce a perfect capsule, all drying off about the middle of April without yielding a grain of drug or good seeds. They thus proved a complete failure in the Meetapore garden.

Section 9: Pussewa: it's Nature and Origin

During the past season the drug produce of the poppy plants under my charge has so abounded with the so-called Pussewa matter that it is very desirable I should offer some remarks on its nature and origin, as there can be no question that its presence involves a large proportionate decrease in pure opium. This indeed is the only natural deteriorative matter, in so far as relates to the pure official drug, if we except, as we should, water, which of course may be either natural or adventitious. Iron indeed has been regarded as a natural constituent of opium. This, I believe, is altogether a mistake. It is evidently a purely adventitious matter, occurring in part from the use of iron scoops (the Government practice in India) in the collection of the drug: from the capsule, as also from the storing of the crude drug in unglazed earthenware dishes. It is from these sources only, as I believe, that iron is present in opium.

In my Manual of Opium Husbandry I gave the following tabular statement of a few analyses of Pussewa which Dr. Sheppard, the then Principal Assistant to the Opium Agent of Benares, was kind enough to send me:

TABLE A

	Consistence	Extractive Matter	Morphine	Narcotine	
1	64.0	50.0	0.5	1.25	O'Shaughnessy
2	85.5	……	2.12	3.38	Eatwell
3	84.75	55.13	1.47	0.9	Sheppard
4	78.75	48.78	1.84	1.87	Sheppard

As the results are given at various degrees of consistency it is well to have them before the eye at a uniform standard. Adopting that of the Behar opium then, we have the results shown in the following tabular statement below:

TABLE B.

	Consistence	Extractive Matter	Morphine	Narcotine	Total Alkaloids
1	70.0	54.06	0.55	1.37	1.92
2	70.0	……	1.73	2.77	4.5
3	70.0	45.53	1.21	0.74	1.95
4	70.0	43.36	1.63	1.66	3.29

For the sake of comparison I will now subjoin tabular statements of the analyses of opium produced by a few of the best varieties cultivated in the gardens here in the seasons 1874-75 and 1876-76:

TABLE C

Variety	Consistence	Extractive Matter	Morphine	Narcotine	Total Alkaloids
Behar Standard	70	47.92	2.69	4.47	7.16
Choura-kutila	70	38.8	3.71	3.71	7.42
Sufaid-danthi	70	35.2	3.36	3.68	7.04
Teyleah	70	37.13	3.16	3.41	6.57
Kala-danthi	70	33.34	2.98	3.4	6.38
Derhi-danthi	70	43.31	3.48	5.03	8.51

Analyst – Dr. Durrant

Variety	Consistence	Extractive Matter	Morphine	Narcotine	Total Alkaloids
Behar Standard	70	43.57	3.17	4.39	7.55
Kala-danthi	70	41.28	2.78	4.94	7.72
Kutila	70	42.26	2.77	4.62	7.39
Teyleah	70	39.76	2.87	4.56	7.43
Sufaid-danthi	70	45.28	2.76	3.59	6.35
Monaria	70	40.45	2.69	4.50	7.19

The following table comprises corresponding results of the analyses of the Malwa, and European opium produce in the gardens during the seasons 1874-75 and 1875-76:

TABLE E

Variety	Consistence	Extractive Matter	Morphine	Narcotine	Total Alkaloids

Behar Standard					
Leela-Malwa	70	45.21	2.64	4.75	7.39
Uggarya-Malwa	70	48.5	3.59	5.98	9.67
Lukria-Malwa	70	49.08	3.18	5.67	8.85
Behar	70	48.92	3.05	5.41	8.48
Standard	70	43.57	3.17	4.39	7.56
Malwa	70	41.79	2.57	5.43	8.00
Red Flower	70	41.67	3.75	4.88	8.63
Spanish Poppy	70	48.96	5.16	6.43	11.59
French Poppy	70	49.59	4.51	4.90	9.41
Italian Poppy	70	45.9	4.06	4.86	8.92
Turkey Poppy	70	48.16	4.10	4.10	8.71

Pussewah is a viscid, black or brownish-black treacle-like liquid which drains more or less copiously from opium in the process of preparation. It gives off a disagreeable mawkish odor, has a nauseous, bitter, and slightly pungent taste, and contains from 64 to 75 per cent, of solid matter. The infusion gives a distinct acid reaction on litmus. Than opium, it is more highly hygroscopic, varying quickly in density with changes in the degree of atmospheric moisture. Relatively to opium it will be observed, from the above tables, to compare favorably as regards "extractive matter" that brown acid substance which has been supposed to form one of the active principles of opium. Again, relatively to opium it is extremely poor in total alkaloids, though it will be observed that in the proportionate development of morphine and narcotine it accords with opium in so far as the latter is somewhat in excess of the former. The results of different analyses are as Dr. Sheppard has informed me, so extremely conflictive that no general deductions could be made from them as to the proportionate development of its basic constituents. These marked variations in the results of analyses of different samples of Pussewah are, as I believe, wholly attributable to variations in the degree of moisture in the soil and the atmosphere during the producing season of the several samples, as affecting the perfect maturation of the opium juices. I would thus explain myself:

There can be no question that Pussewah is a legitimate secretion of the plant, and not merely the result of certain alteration of the opium-juices as they exude from the capsule by the absorption of moisture in damp weather. This it clearly is not, as moisture thus absorbed is readily drained off or evaporated without leaving a trace of Pussewah. On the other hand, if at all present in opium, and not carefully extracted before the final storing of the latter, it is not only always easily detected subsequently, but even in small quantities depreciates much the value of the drug. Now it is well known that the opium produce of naturally damp and strong clayey soils is much more strongly impregnated with the Pussewah impurity than is that from drier and lighter soils, while that from dry, well-drained, light soils exhibits, as a rule, no trace of it. Again Pussewah is always given off most largely by opium when the season is more than averagely moist and cloudy, increasing proportionately with the degree of moisture and shade. On the other hand a dry season, with a clear, heavy atmosphere and bright sunny weather, while most favorable to a copious secretion of pure opium, eliminates or exhausts the Pussewah matter.

Pussewah, therefore, can scarcely be regarded as a distinct or independent secretion, but, on the other hand, and with more truth, it may be regarded as simply a crude, impure, or imperfectly elaborated condition of the opium-juices, the segregation of which is largely due to suppressed respiration and the undue accumulation of watery fluids in the milk vessels. Thus, by avoiding naturally damp and heavy soils and characteristically moist districts for those of a light character and dry atmosphere, we will have a minimum of the Pussewah impurity.

I have been chiefly induced to make the above remarks on the nature of Pussewah and the influence of particular conditions of the soil and the atmosphere on its segregation in the plant from its abounding so largely in the opium produce of the gardens here last season. Thus in the Meetapore gardens, from about 80 seers of opium, there was had no less than eight seers of Pussewah; while in Deegah, from 253 seers of opium, the Pussewah given off amounted to IS seers. The large increase of Pussewah in these gardens for the past season will be better understood when I state that for the season 1875-76 from 427 seers of opium there were only one and a half seers of Pussewah, and for that of 1874-75, 247 seers of opium yielded of Pussewah no more than 2.5 seers. This enormous excess in Pussewah has seriously depreciated the opium returns. I am not prepared to estimate the proportionate loss in the latter, but it must clearly be very large.

Section 10: The Seed Harvest: the Selection of the Capsules and the Storage of the Seed.

We had our seed-harvest in April and May. The weather in April was dry and favorable for the maturation of the capsules. May, however, from occasional and rather heavy showers of rain, and more than an averagely moist atmosphere throughout, was not at all favorable to the storage of the seed.

The first operation is the selection of the most copious drug-producing capsules. This is best and most expeditiously done while the plant is standing, as the primary, secondary, and other capsules, are then readily distinguished, as also the number of drug-yielding incisions. The system practiced here during the past season was, in the first instance, to pick out a few of the most experienced and careful workers for the selection of the best primary or central capsules for the supply of the seeds required next season in the garden under my charge. Now it has been urged that this selective mode involves a considerable amount of extra labor and, of course, expense to the Assamese.

This is a mistake. With hired labor it costs me no more than six annas per beegha to collect the most productive central capsules. These on an average afford one and a half maunds of seed, which, allowing four seers per beegha will afford a sufficiency for fifteen beeghas; that is, equal to about four pies per cottah — certainly a sum over which there can be no grudge.

Moreover, I do not think I exaggerate in assuming that upwards of 75 per cent of the opium cultivation in the two Government agencies is performed by home labor, so that the expenditure of even these few extra pies is not incurred. From five to six maunds only of seed being required for garden use, the best remaining is collected for distribution in the agencies. With this object a second set of work people are charged with the collection of all central and secondary capsules, presenting a minimum of five copious drug-yielding incisions. This incurs on an average double the labor of the first collection, the expense being thus about 12 annas per beegha. The return in seed varies from two to two and a half maunds per beegha. The remaining capsules are gathered promiscuously, and their seeds stored in the godowns along with the smaller sized seeds of the preceding sorts - all being of comparatively little value for crop raising.

From the above statements, then, it is seen that the selection of the capsules as I have recommended really incurs little extra expense, and indeed not more than an hour's extra labor per beegha on the Assamese dependent on home labor.

The selective collection of the capsules being completed, the next operations are the breaking of these and the cleaning of the seeds. Much care is required in preventing mixtures of the different varieties in these operations, and only a few of the most careful workpeople are thus employed. In spite of every care however working with so many sorts and cleaning all with a single set of sieves, I find, for example, occasional plants of red-flowered Malwa amongst the local sorts. This has been remarked by Mr. Masters, Sub-Agent of Hajeepore, who has particularly attended to, and described to me the general characteristics of each variety. He also sent me selected capsules of each as illustrating his descriptive report. I compared these capsules, sample for sample, with those in the gardens here, and the only marked difference was that the latter were nearly all of a much larger size. This in some cases was very marked indeed.

All the residue of the broken capsules and dust having been separated from the seeds by the common hand tools of the natives. Previous to their final storing, I have all sifted in the 1//27th of an inch meshed sieve, with only those which are retained on the sieve being kept for next season's sowing.

For use in the garden I have made a careful selection of seed from the best of each variety. For district distribution I have promiscuously included seeds of the first and second qualities only. In making this selection of seeds for district experiments, I should explain that I had not then received the reports on those distributed last season, otherwise I should have prepared a smaller collection from the first quality only. Last season I distributed in all, between the two Agencies, 42.5 maunds of seed of 13 different samples, in five grades of quality. From the now expressed antipathy of the Assamese to the use of my selected seed, I plainly see I have made a mistake in sending such a large quantity of so many different qualities. It would have been much better to have sent only a small quantity of the first quality. For next season I will keep this in view, and of those now reserved for district distribution I will retain only the largest sized seeds; that is— those which are retained by a sieve with meshes of 1/22nd of an inch on the side of the square. Those distributed last season varied from 1/24th to 1/30th of an inch, and were thus of course all of inferior quality to those which I now purpose to distribute next season. Of this quality the quantity available will be from eight to ten maunds only for each Agency.

After the separation of all the smaller sized seeds from the larger, the latter are mixed with pounded camphor and placed in well-burned earthenware vessels, which contain from ten to twenty seers each. Prior to closing them up with a strong tenacious clay, the surface of the seeds is again sprinkled over with pounded camphor, which proves an effective preventive to the attacks of various seed-eating grubs and insects that affect and seriously injure untreated poppy seeds in their store-pots.

The seeds for distribution in the Agencies last season were sent to the Agents respectively on the 22nd and 26th of September. I observe, however, that the Sub-Agents have in certain cases received them too late for the allotment of the better soils fur experiments, to which they attribute the unsatisfactory returns. I shall therefore this season, if the weather is at all favorable, endeavor to have the supply for each Agency sieved as above, packed, and prepared for dispatch by the middle of September. They should thus reach their destinations in time for the first sowings.

Section 11: The Diseases and Injuries of the Crop, by Parasitic Fungi, Insects, etc.

(Author's note: although written well over 100 years ago this section of Scott's work still stands as the standard reference for pests and diseases of the Opium Poppy.)

Opium, as affected by weather, is, like indigo, a most uncertain crop. There is this difference between them, however, that the latter is most liable to injury from the germinative stage to the acquiring of the fourth or fifth leaf. Opium, on the other hand, though susceptible to unfavorable conditions of weather in the earlier stages of the plant's growth, is eminently affected by weather at the later stages of development, and especially from the appearance of the flower-bud until the capsule has attained its full size and the milky fluid properly matured. Then, again, all being favorable up to and through these stages, there remains the period for the collection of the drug, which, as regards weather influence, is perhaps the most precarious of all. For example a hail-storm of a few minutes' duration will utterly ruin the plant as an opium producer; then, again, a shower of rain between the periods of capsule scarification and collection of the drug incurs the loss of a portion of the whole of the day's return. This is serious, as according to the varying fertility of the crop it involves from a third to the fifth of the gross produce. Opium is thus really one of the most critical and precarious of crops, though upon the whole less liable than many other agricultural and garden crops to special diseases.

The garden crop during the past season suffered mainly from gangrene. This was, no doubt, a result of the unusual moistness of the season, and naturally was most prevalent on the lower and wetter portion of the garden. With several varieties of the local poppy, however, it never assumed other than a sporadic character, isolated plants suddenly dying off in all stages of development. On the other hand, with the European varieties it obtained quite an epidemic character, large patches of hitherto apparently healthy plant giving way to it. This was particularly marked in the sunny intervals in cloudy and moist weather, the first symptoms being the drooping of the leaves and the tips of the branches, all rapidly under the sun's rays becoming brown and withered; while black gummy matters exude more or less copiously from the stem - the plant of course dies. Further than avoiding naturally heavy, damp and ill-drained soils, nothing really can be done to check poppy gangrene. It is well to uproot duly all affected plants, as the disease is readily communicable by the roots.

In previous reports I have noticed and described under the name of scleriasis a peculiar affection of the poppy, characterized by the hardening, so to speak, of the whole outer tissues of the plant, and the utter arrest of the drug secretions. I have shown that such cases of functional derangement are very prevalent in the local crops from unselected seed, and consequently cause serious deterioration to the crop. I have also shown that the disease or affection is hereditary, that is that a large percentage of the progeny are similarly affected and I have urged, and myself practiced, the uprooting of plants so affected. The result is extremely satisfactory, as during the past season I have scarcely observed a single scleriatic plant.

Petechia, another hereditary disease seriously deteriorative to the secretion of drug, noticed as very prevalent, has also all but disappeared from my garden crops. This result has been gradually attained from year to year by the careful extraction of all affected plants.

Broomrapes (the tkokra of the natives), which practically affect the roots of the poppy, etc. proved rather troublesome during the past season in the Meetapore gardens. The seeds of these plants are so extremely minute that a breath of air will widely distribute them, and no doubt their prevalence on the poppy during the past season is due to dissemination from the adjoining gardens, where I have observed that they abounded on the brinjals and tomatoes! I was careful, however, to have all uprooted as they made their appearance, so that they did no apparent injury to the crop, though of coarse causing not a little extra labor.

The most serious parasitic foe of the opium poppy, however, is a blight mould technically known as Peronospora arborescens, which is always more or less common on the plant in one or other of its modes of development. I have described at length in my Opium Manual and previous reports the vegetative and reproductive economy of this mould as affecting the opium poppy. I have also shown how differences in the degree of oxygenation of the juices can promote, suppress, or impede the development of the mould. These observations indicate, as I believe, the only really practical and effective mode in which we may contend with the mould and relieve the poppy from one of its periodical scourges.

For the season just closed, I first observed the mould on the earliest sown crops of the Meetapore gardens in the beginning of November. I found it not infrequent on the cotyledon leaves in the first instance, and by the middle of the month it had appeared on the first cycle of normal leaves.

From casual observations on plants from seeds steeped in camphorated water, and alluded to in my Opium Manual (vide page 36), I repeated these experiments. The seeds immediately, prior to their being sown, were thoroughly soaked with camphorated water and dried in a powder of quicklime and wood ashes. This treatment much accelerated germination and invigorated the young plant, but in no marked way did it prevent or modify the development of the mould on the leaves. Trusting to the camphorated water alone, I did not repeat experiments with the alcohol and camphor solution. In my previous year's experiments the results were so far unsatisfactory that the seeds germinated sparingly and tardily, and the young plant was not at all healthy. This, however, I attribute to the strength of the steeps, I having used a saturated solution of strong alcohol. The use of a low proof spirit with less camphor might afford very different results. In the approaching season I purpose making experiments with seeds so treated.

I carefully observed the development and extension of the mould in the Deegah and Meetapore crops. I particularly noted that though abounding on the plants in both gardens, it extended from the lower to the upper series of leaves much less actively than in the previous season when I have had it under my eye. This am disposed to attribute to the quantity and conditions of the plant's juices. I have already explained my grounds for this belief, attributing it to the more than average moisture of the season and suppressed transpiration of watery fluids from the plant. This abnormal condition of the plant's juices is thus very probably the cause of the comparatively slow extension of the mould, as observed, from the lower to the upper leaves. The observation is anyhow of much practical and theoretical interest, as indicating the mode in which we may alone successfully contend with the poppy mould, as indeed all others affecting the inner tissues of plants that is by aiming at the alteration of the foster plant's juices by chemical applications to the soil. I do not doubt that by continued experiments in this direction we may yet be able to ameliorate at least, if not altogether suppress, those hitherto immitigable devastators of our crops. I have specially urged this in my Opium Manual {vide page 159, et seq.) and I shall venture to express the hope that the duty deputed me, in the first instance by the Government of India, and subsequently cordially participated in by the Government of Bengal, under two late Lieutenant-Governors, may be continued until I have fully substantiated the views I have advanced on the modes of suppressing these parasitic pests of our crops. I regret much that it should be at all contemplated to discontinue, or reduce in any way, my experimental work just now, when most important results are most likely to accrue.

But to return to the subject of the extension of the mould from the lower to the upper leaves of the plant, I have to observe that in more than average dry seasons this is affected by the close of January, and on an average at latest by the middle of February. Well, in the unusually moist season now closed, the uppermost series of leaves scarcely showed a trace of the mould at the latter date, and indeed were only very slightly marked with it a month later, when the generality of the plant had all but ceased to yield opium and beginning to mature its seeds. Moreover, to the last the mould patches on the undivided leaves were to the last smaller and more isolated than in any of the few preceding seasons during which I have observed it. For all this, however, it abounded on the plants; but this fortunately in the fertile or spare bearing mode of development, which, as I have shown, causes little apparent injury to the poppy. In the sterile and truly blight form it last affected the poppy in the season 1874-75, this being preceded again by that of 1870-7 1, that is in an interval of four seasons. From data given in previous reports and in my - Manual of Opium Husbandry there is every reason to believe that its recurrence in the blight form varies from three to five years. Now, from the peculiar and tardy development in the past season it is very probable that it may not, as I had feared from its prevalence on the preceding season's plant (vide Manual, page 168), appear in a virulent form next season, but especially if the latter is a dry season there is likelihood of its not assuming the blight form in the crops of 1878-79. I by no means make this statement with any alarmist views, but simply on conviction by personal observations and other data illustrative of the periodical occurrence of this mould in a more or less virulent blight form.

I pass on to the insect foes of the opium poppy. These fortunately are not numerous, in so far as regards the growing plants nor even dangerous if early and proper repressive measures are adopted.

The following only call for notice here as affecting last season's garden crops:

The first is the caterpillar of a dart-moth (apparently of the genus noctua) which attacks the young plant. This last season all the earlier sown plants escaped it, the later sown crops only being attacked, and this in the last week of November. Freely dusting the plants in the evening, however, with a powdery mixture in about equal parts of quicklime and ashes, the ravages of the caterpillar were effectively prevented. The attacks of this caterpillar, I may remark, are confined almost wholly to the very early stages of the plant's growth, and this, from a suggestion of Mr. Darwin, previously noticed, I believe, is wholly due to the blandness of the plant's juices at that period, the pungent and nauseous milk-sap of the more advanced plant effectively defending it from all such unwelcome guests.

Crickets were very troublesome for a short time in several plots about the middle of September. They are not quite so easily kept in check as the above caterpillar, continuing their depredatory visits in spite of a liberal application of lime and ashes. Quicklime alone in a fine powder is an effective preventive however, as is also a mixture in about equal parts of that and soot. The mode of use is simply to dust the young plants freely with either one or the other about sunset. One, or at the most two applications will be sufficient.

Again, when the poppy is fully developed and the seeds about to mature, another caterpillar of the genus noted above {noctua) makes its appearance and feeds on the seeds.

In the plates accompanying my annual report for 1873-74 I have given colored figures of both species in the caterpillar and moth states. I have also alluded to the fact that it was after the drug had been all but exhausted from the capsule that the latter caterpillar began its depredations, penetrating the capsule and devouring the seeds. In the Manual I have indeed remarked that "it is interesting to observe that the caterpillars carefully avoid the younger and drug-containing capsules, the milky juice of which, as I know from experiment, has a strong narcotic influence on them, this for some little time being preceded by quick convulsive-like twitchings, etc. We have thus another proof of the milky sap of the poppy being a means of protecting it from the visits of unwelcome guests as Mr. Darwin suggests.

The maturing poppy has here another most troublesome visitor in the common rose-ringed parrakut, the soogha or lotha of the natives. This is a most daring depredator; lighting on any trees adjoining the crop and darting as opportunity arises on the largest and most conspicuous capsules which it cuts off and carries away. If not watched they simply settle on the plant and deliberately shell out and devour the seeds, causing much damage.

APPENDIX TWO: TRADITIONAL USES OF CANNABIS, OPIUM AND COCA

Opium, Coca, Cannabis & Folk Medicine

While it is unlikely that anyone would be at a loss at what to do with a fine crop of hemp, coca or poppies, it is probably also true that there exist numerous souls whose tastes run to the slightly more adventurous realm of experimentation. In this section we'll look at a few of the more interesting variations on the basic theme of the drugs as expressed in various concoctions, medicinal as well as gourmet.

Andean Indians and their Poporo

Several times a day he sits down, takes some leaves, puts them one by one into his mouth and rolls them into an *aculio* (quid), adding a little *llipla* (lime) which he takes from his ever present *poporo*. The *poporo* is a little gourd, bored at the mouth on the upper part, in which the Indian keeps his *llipta*. This *llipta* is a white powder composed of ashes of vegetables and of calcified shells pulverized, with which the consumers of Coca have been accustomed, from the most remote times, to season their quid. It is, really, an alkaline substance intended to isolate the different elements of the leaf and to make the action of the Coca more prompt.

The consumption of Coca by children is strictly prohibited. The children, quite naturally, do not obey this rule and thus Coca is apt to appear to them all the sweeter because it is forbidden. But nearly always their breath, charged with the tell-tale odor of Coca, betrays them on parents, and the latter make them pay for the pleasure which they have stolen, and to which they are not entitled until they are of age, with very severe chastisement. Only when they have grown up will they be allowed to chew Coca and to carry the *poporo,* which they then do not relinquish even in the grave.

On coming of age the young Indian is consigned to an old woman, who keeps him a few hours in her hut to initiate him in mysteries of man's estate. After this ceremony she gives him the *chuspa* (Coca pouch), invests him with the *poporo* and consecrates him a *coquero.* One should see with what pride the novitiate leaves the threshold of the cabin, which he entered as a child a few hours before and from which he departs a man, that is to say, carrying the *chuspa* and the *poporo,* and able to chew with impunity, before old people, this precious leaf which had been forbidden him until then.

No privilege is comparable to his! See with what an important air he draws forth the Coca leaves from his *chuspa,* as he rolls them in his palms to make a large quid of them, which he then conveys to his mouth, moistens delightingly with saliva, and places under his jaws and against his cheeks. He is seen holding carefully in right hand little stick, the of which he is to moisten by putting it into his mouth, and which he will dip into the *poporo* in order that the *llipta* may adhere to its moistened part. He carefully carries the part of his little stick covered with ll*ipta* to his quid, and thus performs the operation of mixing the alkaline powder with the masticated leaf.

It is at this moment that the quid of Coca affords the young adult the most delightful sensations. His jaws munch it slowly, his tongue collects rolls it up against the left cheek, all the *papillae* of his mouth refresh themselves deliciously with the soothing and aromatic juices of the precious leaf, and by the slow and measured motions of deglutition, he carries with delight the precious liquid into the pharynx and thence to the stomach. While he is accomplishing this important operation, his eyes swim with beatitude, over his entire countenance is diffused an expression of content and unutterable joy, and his right hand slowly turns the little stick around the upper part of the *poporo,* where are deposited little by little the *llipta* and masticated Coca, which on leaving his mouth adhere to its extremity.

The only occupation of the first days of the adult is the much-loved quid of Coca and the encrusting of his gourd, which we cannot do better than compare to the crusting of the tobacco pipe, with this that our confirmed smokers blacken hundreds of their pipes during their existence, while the Indian encrusts only one gourd in his whole life; so that by the thickness of the crust formed around a *poporo*, it is possible to judge the age of its owner· This which hardly ever exceeds the thickness of a ring on the *poporo* of a young Indian, ends by reaching the dimension of a large mushroom on the *poporo* of an old man.

The crust is produced by the particles of Coca and *llipta* mixed with saliva which are deposited little by little about the mouth of the *poporo* by smearing with the stick. These deposits are brought about in an almost imperceptible manner. It is only after some months that the surface of the *poporo,* on which the chewer continually turns the little stick, becomes covered with a hardly perceptible layer of calcareous substance; at the end of two or three years the superimposed layers form a ring which grows larger from year to year, and which finally attains the thickness we have spoken of above.

As we have said before, the Indian never parts with his *poporo,* let him be awake or asleep, at home or on his travels, the *poporo* is always attached to his belt. An Indian would part with all he holds most dear in the world, all, before parting with his *poporo.*

Coca Leaf Tea & America's Morbid Obesity

As you read through the 18th & 19th century medical literature on Coca you are immediately struck by how many remedies for weight-related problems there are. Coca leaf tea has many properties, but the combination of suppressing appetite while at the same time giving immense energy and stamina appears quite frequently in the literature. In fact, sipping Coca leaf tea became a favorite Victorian way of controlling weight among the fashionable ladies of Europe. Now, while it may be a gross simplification to believe that anything as elegantly simple as coca leaf tea could offer a solution to American obesity, the fact is that if severely overweight people had access to this mildly stimulating, refreshing herb tea they could very likely do away with all the diet pills, surgeries, and fad diets and simply get their appetites under control with a few cups of this natural medicine every day. Of course this solution puts at risk vast industries that rely on an ever-increasing supply of obese Americans to support their balance sheets, so it is very unlikely that the coca leaf tea solution will ever get a tryout. However, I can see in the not so distant future a weight loss resort being founded in, say, Cuzco, where obese Americans can check in for a month or so of coca tea, light meals, and long walks in the mountain air, after which they will be able to return home and show off their new 'me' to their friends and family who are still stuck in their bloated bodies. Maybe after a few hundred fat Americans went to Peru for the coca leaf tea cure and came back slim and energized there would be a beginning awareness of the health potential of this awesome medicine!

Opium Delights

Here are four interesting recipes for use of Opium in cases of medical complaints. One never finds Opium compounded with other items for use strictly as a high, except where it forms a minor base for the addition of strong herbs such as aconite, nux vomica, hellebore or datura, a practice generally limited to addicts at the very low end of the food chain in Asian countries. For the most part the Chinese, who are the people with the deepest historical interest in Opium, had little to do with the use of Opium in such stone concoctions.

In the case of nausea and vomiting, a drink made from Poppy seeds in the following manner will be useful. Three-tenths of a pint of the seeds of the White Poppy, three-tenths of an ounce of powdered ginseng, and a five-inch section of the yellow yam are to be cut and ground fine. Boil the mixture in 2 3/10 pints of pure water. Take of this six-tenths of a pint and add to it a little syrup of raw ginger and a pinch of fine sea salt. Mix well and take early and late in the day.

Su Sung Sung Dynasty

For asthmatic cough, with perspiration, in both summer and winter months, take 2 1/2 ounces of whole ripe poppy capsule, removing stem and outer membrane. Simmer in rice vinegar. Take one ounce of the liquor and mix well with 1/2 ounce of black plums. Heat slowly and then pulverize. Take a dose of 2/10 ounce for several days, whenever needed, with hot water.

Liu Ho-chien Chin Dynasty

For pain above or below the diaphragm take 21/2 ounces of opium, one ounce of asafoetidia, 1/2 ounce of aloes and 1/4 ounce of cow bezoar. The last three of the ingredients are pulverized together. Heat the opium with a bit of hot water until dissolved. Mix the whole with enough honey to achieve a firm texture, and roll into pills the size of small beans. Wrap in gold leaf. When the body is hot, take with cold water; when chilled, take with hot water.

Li Shih-chen Ming Dynasty

For asthma, rheumatism or pain in the heart, take the poppy capsule when ripe, remove the stalk and outer skin and the string inside fibres. Let the capsule dry in a dark place, and then cut very small. Mix well with rice vinegar, honey, black plums and orange peel. Of the whole make small pills, and take as needed.

Kung Sin Ming Dynasty

Cannabis Preparations

Here are some interesting, easily prepared variations on the use of Cannabis. For others, please see The Connoisseur's Handbook of Marijuana which I wrote some years ago, in which I present a section on Cannabis cookery. (NB – also since this book was first written in 1974 I published the Marijuana Foods Handbook in 1981 – full of recipes and directions for extracting Cannabis with various substrates.)

Therapeutic Butter

A method of preparing hashish which comes down from at least five hundred years ago in India and Egypt consists of taking the fresh flowering tops of Cannabis, removing the stems and beating out the seeds, and straining through a fine mesh screen. The resulting powder is then mixed with an equal weight of butter, and approximately 1/10 by weight of cold water is added. The water does not enter into solution; its function is to carry away heat by evaporation during the cooking process.

The mixture is to be cooked over very low heat for a period of 11/2 hours per pound of mass, after which the resulting grey-green mixture is chilled. After the mass solidifies, take a butter whisk or, if available, an electric mixer and homogenize the mixture which will, in the process, take on a yellowish tinge.

Hashish butter was used extensively as a general sedative in both Eqyptian and Indian medical systems, but recommended dosages varied from 0.5 grams per 24 hour period to 3-5 grams every twelve hours depending, no doubt, upon both the severity of the symptoms being treated and the generosity of nature of the prescribing physician.

The Composted Marijuana of Sind

A little-known delicacy which may appeal to lovers of Camembert cheese, chocolate-covered ants and Ambergris comes to us from the upper Sind area of the Himalayas. Here Cannabis is prepared by burying the flowering tops of freshly harvested plants in a pit four to five feet deep and several feet across, the whole mass of tops covered with a generous layer of fresh goat dung and live coals piled on top of the dung.

The pit is allowed to bake slowly for two to three weeks, and only the faintest of fires maintained among the coals on top. Some villages substitute hot rocks for live coals, changing the rocks perhaps twice a day.

After the two or three week waiting period, when the heat, vapor and juices have done their work, the petrified dung layer is shoveled aside and the coagulated and slightly stiff flower spikes removed. The most smokable little pods of resin and flower are picked off each spike. These pods are then crushed flat in the palms, the little mass heated a bit in a clay jar thrust into coals, formed into small cakes and thus made ready for a bit of heady smoking.

Turkish Coffee Cake

To prepare this little delicacy, one takes a quantity of the finest esrar, or powder of first quality, and places it in an iron pan over a brazier with low heat. Once a strong, heavy odor begins to rise from the mass, which will begin to agglutinate, you plunge your hands into a bowl containing a very strong, thick, sweet Turkish coffee and immediately scoop up the slightly hot and somewhat melted powder from the pan. You then knead the mass with your hands on a slab of cold marble, repeating the application of coffee until you have a lump the consistency of dough, coffee-colored and with the odor of coffee overriding that of the Cannabis.

Once you have the cake at a pleasing consistency, color and odor, it can be made up into little morsels whose weight is ordinarily about 4 grams. These cakes are usually preserved by wrapping in slightly moist linen and storing them in a cool place. The man from whose report we gather this little recipe, a Dr. Mongeri, notes that "One of these little cakes alone is sufficient to plunge the uninitiated into a full ecstacy."

Preparation of Halwa

This is a specialty of the Dravidian area of southern India. Take several ounces of flowering tops and boil them in two pints or so of sorghum syrup for about twenty minutes. The mixture is then poured through a coarse cloth, and that which is trapped by the cloth is kept, and the residue thrown away. The filtrate is then mixed with approximately equal parts of flour and butter, and often supplemented to taste with almond paste. The mixture is rolled out flat, cut into squares and let dry.

In some places the filtrate is treated differently. After being collected, it is fried in butter, and during cooking saffron and almonds are added. After it has been fried down to a firm consistency, it is allowed to cool and then cut into bite-size pieces.

Preparation of Bhang

Bhang is the most popular of the traditional preparations of Cannabis for drinking, and is used in all parts of India. The basic drink is prepared by taking Bhang - the lower leaves of the Cannabis plant and pounding them in a mortar or bowl along with a little black pepper and sugar, to taste, and then diluting the mixture with hot or cold water to the desired strength. There are, however, a great many variations on this basic recipe.

Upon many occasions one finds that in addition to the bhang-pepper-sugar mixture, an interesting flavor is created by the addition of almonds, milk curds and aniseed. Other ingredients often added, depending on the part of India you are visiting and the social and economic class of your host, include melon, poppy or cucumber seeds; rose petals; or the spices saffron, cardamom or cloves. In many cases, an extract of various herbs is added; most commonly one encounters extract of asafetida, licorice and senna. Then too, the addition of various fruit juices is considered de rigueur in many places, in particular the juice of pomegranate, coconut and date are favored.

Preparation of Manzoul

The basic vehicle for this confection is achieved by mixing Hashish with sesame oil and cocoa butter in a ratio of 1:5:5. This starter mixture is worked into a thick paste, and often a bit of powdered sweet chocolate is added. Then, depending on the tastes of the maker, one of three combinations of spices and herbs are added. In the first instance, one finds a mixture of celery, quince, cress and onion seeds added to the basic preparation. Secondly, one commonly finds a mixture of cloves, cinnamon, cardamom, nutmeg, ginger and black pepper utilized. Lastly, one encounters Manzoul with a mixture of almonds, walnuts, hazelnuts, pistachio and pine-nuts ground together and added to taste.

The Manzoul thus fortified with taste-enhancing and reputedly aphrodisiacal goodies is rolled onto a flat surface and cut into small cubes and disks, which are to be chewed slowly and swallowed.

Preparation of Garawish Candy

One part powdered Hashish is mixed with four parts well-thickened sorghum syrup, one part raw Opium and one-half part Datura Stramonium (or Jimson Weed). The basic mix is flavored to taste with chocolate, cloves, vanilla, cinnamon, cardamom, nutmeg, etc., and cooked very slowly over a low fire until it thickens to a near-solid paste. The paste is then poured onto a cool, oiled marble slab, where it is rolled out in slab form to a thickness of 1/4_1/2" After it cools it is cut into cubes, which are frequently wrapped gaily in bright paper or foil and offered as presents on festive occasions.

Preparation of Dawamesk

Take these ingredients in the following ratios: Walnut meat, almond meats, flowering tips of Cannabis, and honey -10 parts; nutmeg, mild black pepper, and pistachio meats -2.5 parts; Datura seeds, Belladonna berries, and butter - .5 parts. Mix the butter and honey. Pulverize and mix all other ingredients. Blend the two mixtures, and place the Dawamesk in a closed earthenware jar to season for at least a week in a cool, dry place. Dawamesk is normally eaten with a spoon, and the usual dose is two teaspoons full after the heavy meal of the day.

Preparation of Charas Dates

Prepare a paste of almonds, pistachios and sugar. Add powdered hashish to taste. Remove the pits from fresh, firm dates, and replace with a stuffing of the paste.

APPENDIX THREE: A COMMENTARY ON THE BEING ELECTRIC

(NB – this little essay drew a lot of reader comments in the original International Cultivators Handbook, so at the risk of taking you too far into the crystals & rainbows timeframe of the 70s, I am leaving it in this updated edition.)

This commentary is, in some ways, very different from the subject matter of this book, yet there is a natural flow from a concern with the drug experience and its biological components to a concern with the nature of the life experience and its perceptual corollaries. I've noticed that the drug experience, when it is not creating problems for people, is for many a part of living which is full of wonder. Perceptions which derive from the drug experience are not normally useful in constructing evidence in the accepted western scientific mode; however, the windows on life experience which can be opened through drugs often lead to insights and understandings which yield a strong sense of being.

With this commentary I want to share some of my continuing sense of wonder at the ways in which life may be questioned. The drug experience so often affords one a chance to discard, for the moment at least, whole fields of assumptions about the way things are. This in turn leads to the sensing of the fascinating satisfaction which people feel when they are free to ask - "What if... ?" I am here wanting to share with fellow explorers of space, and time, and life, some of my what ifs. I hope that some valuable energy is released, and that some people will find this material useful in integrating parts of their own deep perceptual fields.

In short, I think that this commentary will make this book about drugs a better book. I hope that's so.

It is apparently an incontrovertible necessity that life's flow begin at the sub-cellular levels of material organization. There is a microcosmic drama enacted at these sub-levels which is imperceptible, even to the instruments of our complex mind, which is capable of directing probes through so many greater and lower levels of universal organization, seeking to detect the origin of its being. Even should technicians succeed in creating life - that is, in creating the material organization necessary for the initiation of the process - the question of the origin of the flow of life will not be answered.

Why does the scheme of life require that it begin always at remote and inaccessible levels? Rather, what is it which occurs on these levels which is never again duplicated at higher levels of material organization? We give the unnamable a name - the beginning of life - but peer as we will we cannot seem to break the vital snares which bind our vision.

Does life begin? Or does it flow into being and manifestation. That is, does life become whatever it is as we see it through a series of events in a material universe which is as we see it, or does life flow into channels which we account for with our assumptions about a physical universe, already defined as an entity in some universal context unaccounted for in our assumptions about the natural order. Because we are of life does not necessarily mean that we have a proprietary understanding of its nature. It is at least possible that we are mis-ordering some of our assumptions about the way things are, and mistaking other assumptions.

So - we can either assume that life is of this universe and strive to discover its nature, or we can assume that life is of another universe, plane or dimension, and work to penetrate that mystery with our mind; or, we can assume that it is not necessarily the nature of life which is hidden, rather it is that the flaws in our perception, which are unknown to us, and which may therefore appear to be that which they conceal.

If we grant that these unknown flaws in our perception, if they exist, may vary from individual to individual, then there is a good chance that these flaws can be discovered. The process would be somewhat like the construction of an astronomical parallax. In much the same way that a near astronomical object can be seen to move against the background of the stars when viewed from two positions, flaws in perception may be seen to move against the background of assumptions when viewed from adequately separated positions. The ability to do this can be one of the valuable attributes of a positive drug experience.

Drugs can be a tool of being in alternative, which is not necessarily to say higher states of consciousness. They are only one of many such tools - granted - and they are deceptively easy, often pleasant tools to use, but nevertheless the drug experience has been, for many, the source of that light which illuminates the nature and place of being in a heretofore darkly shadowed universe. Each to his own drug experience, as each to his own life and death, but as with living and dying, despite the remorseless individuality of the experience, people still can share a common knowledge and understanding of an undertaking which is the province of each solitary soul.

There is a word. It is short, and ugly, and as superficial as many things today; yet there is an image behind the word, an image rarely used because it is too sensitive and too personal. The word is trip. The image is search. In our time drugs have come bursting upon a generation of people whose confusion may be unparalleled; yet the image of search is old, and reasserts itself in every time of darkness. For myself and for many, many people the search has taken on new forms, reflected in our lives. The drug experience, formative in subtle ways, is clarifying both the process and the object of that search.

Carl Jung said that all of man's strivings have been directed toward the consolidation of consciousness. Ego is the source of misdirection, thus failure in the search for consolidation. Ego is the insinuating snare, the distraction preventing integration of experience personal and experience universal. Achievement of perspective on ego is a necessary step in the search for unity, and the drug experience, while too often destroying ego has been, for many, the energy flow to ego-transcendence, the snare-break yielding a consciousness free to seek unrealized forms of unity.

The drug experience provides tools for insight into the second level of search, the search for awareness of place. Because of our sensate nature, habits of thought and perception arise which are the derivative of our organism's idiosyncrasies. Many of these thought habits are projected upon the physical nature of the world and universe; we grow to believe that all is as we perceive it to be because we learn early to trust our ability to perceive truly. The search for place is so often misdirected and cancelled by this characteristic human error. Through the drug experience, many people learn that what is perceived as the universe and world of space and time are quite different at different levels of awareness; at least, the perceptions are quite different.

Consider the creatures that we are. Our whole consciousness is hemispherical. We look out from our brain through two eyes which scan an arc of 90° from a point directly in front of our nose. The nose, the mouth and the two ears are forward-facing organs on the front face of a spherical skull which sits upon a column of flesh and bone designed to turn through an arc of 1800. The rest of our body, though upon occasion capable of 360° rotation of function, is basically oriented to the forward hemisphere described by our senses, and the head, oddly enough, is the least adaptable to dealing with the full circle of possibilities. The person-creature looking out from this body is so oriented to the concept of forward that most of his perceptual, and many of his conceptual activities are unconsciously so oriented as well. We are almost never aware of the rear hemisphere of our mind, or our universe.

Our creature-born limitations are natural enough, they just aren't, in normal experience, sufficiently obvious to allow us to work them through to new levels of perception. We do not see that infinity works all ways because we do not see all ways. Our minds are trained by fellow creatures, equally ignorant, into patterns of seeing which do not allow us to deal with a whole framework within which to build awareness upon experience. The mind which works to grasp or accept the idea of FORWARD and UP rarely goes on to work through the concepts of DOWN and BACK.

In the heart of our unexamined selves we come to believe in particular levels of the universe, and in our incorporation therein. We recognize that there are physical things smaller than our senses can directly detect, as well as larger. But while we are quite capable of peering up and forward and accepting an infinite space and time, we spend vast energies, whether of investigation or pure belief, in peering downward looking for a final floor upon which to plant our feet and our flag. As a baby fears falling our minds fear a universe without foundation, and we work to erect massive bases of law and belief, to establish a final reference point for our physical being, from which it may be conclusively stated that mankind is a matter of creatures, so long, so wide, and so deep, standing finally upon a subatomic stage looking OUT at a universe which goes UP, flowing through a time which goes FORWARD. That seems, our senses and our fears insist, to be the way things work. But the mystical experience, and the drug experience offers access to that experience, says no. In that experience we find that what is known, as opposed to what is believed, is that we are a distinctive bundle of something we call life, with a refinement we call intellect, occupying a level of physical states called existence, within which we detect a particular state called being, which cannot be tied firmly to any particular immutable point in any particular immutable time, and which is without ties to any universal absolute because here there is no fundament. Those who come to know this, whether through the drug experience or through any other form of perceptual integration, are discovering that which has been blocking the next stages in the evolutionary history of human beings. Now, am I Chuang Tzu who has dreamed that he was a butterfly? Or, am I a butterfly which is now dreaming that it is Chuang Tzu?

I like to work with the idea that life might well flow into what we call our universe. Our universe is defined by our perceptions and their conceptual offspring. Our perceptions are expandable, therefore at any moment they are limited. Any expanded perception has the potential for moving you closer to an understanding of the nature of life, because life comes from the unknown into the known, and moves off again.

Our senses are organ responses to contact with objects of varying solidity, and with the ebb and flow of heat energy in the world; to the intake of chemical compounds; to the elastic modulation of air pressure waves; to the electromagnetic storms which sweep in from the stars. Our organs have developed through time in response to the needs of the organizing properties of the nervous system, and in general proportion to the intensity and character of manifestations of local physical phenomena of our universe of matter. But does our particular set of organs exhaust the possibilities for responding to and monitoring all universal phenomena? We might reasonably conclude that if other sorts of universal phenomena existed, we would have organs capable of responding to them at some point in their range. Well, we do have a great many organs, and it seems to be that we have been somewhat arbitrary in our decisions about what was sensory and what was not. For instance.

We conceive of the brain as an organizer of the impulses sent along by our ears, eyes, nose and so forth, but it is possible (is it not?) that the organizing functions of the brain are secondary to, or at least separable from its function as a sensory organ, but that because of the distracting character of some of the brain's peripheral manifestations the personality, for instance - we are unaware that it is possible to perceive the universal phenomenon, or phenomena, to which the brain is sensate?

It is understandable that we do not treat the brain as a sense organ, if that it is. It is probably as simple as the fact that the brain is not an outside organ like the eyes and ears, and we think of sense organs and sensory impressions as being outside phenomena. This body-fortress assumption is probably as old as awareness, and makes primitive sense. Yet a simple reversal of assumption about our placement - that we are within the universe, and possibly of universes, and not simply in the universe - allows us to consider the possibility that the brain has developed in response to phenomena as valid as waves and particles.

It is interesting to look around for what might be the phenomena to which a sensate brain would be attuned. Psychic and metaphysical phenomena present the most obvious areas of inquiry. But what are they? It seems reasonable that they may be idiosyncratic human manifestations of the involvement of the mind with states within which matter is conditional, states which lie within and flow from another universe, from which life also flows. In this sense, it may be that the brain is our organism's sensory monitor for life origin and destiny. In fact, the brain may well be our organism's provision for the monitoring of life's discreet manifestations by the primal state of life. The evolution of the physical brain, generation after generation through eons, is a story of the development, first, of a sense of function, then a sense of selfhood and, then, with the human brain, the beginnings of a sense of being.

In the science of awareness, which is philosophy, the sense of oneness is considered the next step, the transmutation of awareness of being into a next-higher state. If life strives, then brain evolution makes sense when seen in these terms.

If we are able to treat the life force as a phenomenon as distinct in its own way as light or heat, then we must be able to look for the universal context within which this force is generated and manifested. It seems clear that while life is manifested in the molecular universe, it is not of that universe - that is, it does not register on any instruments which deal with molecular phenomena. The life force seems to be a wholly non-molecular phenomenon. So maybe it makes sense to talk about two universes, in the sense that we know that there are at least two kinds of forces. (It also seems to me that the life force is apparently not the only non-molecular phenomenon which we see manifested in the molecular universe, but for the moment let's look at what seem to be some of the characteristics of the life force, insofar as it shows itself to us by virtue of its molecular manifestation.)

In a very heavy book, Biology & The Future Of Man, a symposium edited by Philip Handler (Oxford University Press, 1970) it is said that 'Life is not one of the fundamental categories of the universe, like matter, energy and time, but is a manifestation of certain molecular combinations". (p.165).

But have we established so completely what matter, energy and time are that we can call them fundamental categories of the universe? What universe? Hadn't we better call them provisional attributes of our understanding about certain levels of perception and operation?

The definition of life as a manifestation of certain molecular combinations tells us very little about life; rather, it speculates on life's temporal locale. It may well be a mistake to look for the definition of life in the body of the living organism, for a lot of what seem to me to be pretty good reasons.

Clearly, the force of life is breathed into each organism-to-be at only one point in a time-defined molecular universe. Equally clearly, each life manifestation is a new organism - there is no intact resurrection of previously living organisms which have at some point lost life. Also, life enters into only certain specialized molecular aggregates - life is not breathed randomly into just any old agglomeration of dust.

In the case of sexually reproducing organisms, it might be argued that the sperm and egg are living pieces of matter, but I think that it is more beautiful than that. The process of fertilization is the bringing together of molecular material which is life in potential only. The egg without the sperm is charged with a readiness for life, as is the sperm without the egg. But until they combine their molecular potential, there seems to be no living. True, there is motion, but it seems to be motion in search of life; there is a dynamism of matter of extraordinarily high potential acting under the impetus of the energies of their parent organism. To use an image, the sperm and egg are non-living molecular bundles which borrow, for an extremely short span, primitive life energies of their parent organisms in order that they may realize an individual life manifestation, but this individualized manifestation does not become a conduit for the life force until the bundles fuse, satisfying the 'complex, singular requirements of the life force for particular entry conditions in the molecular universe. It is almost as if sexual reproduction is a valve which assures that the life force is not indiscriminately tapped by the geometrically increasing nature of asexual reproduction, which characterizes only those organisms of very low individual magnitude on the scale of intensity of the force's manifestation.

Individual organismic life commences with the fusion of critical molecular components. As this fusion occurs, the life force is tapped, flows into and uniquely activates a special piece of the molecular universe. Fission then takes place in the molecular aggregate, first resulting in a duplicating series of cell division which may simply expand the storage capacity of the organism for the flow of life energy which has been initiated and which quickly becomes a powerful flood. Later, fission begins to produce specialized sets of cell-division series which result in the functional components of the organism. Life on earth is distinguished, one kind from another, largely by these diversifying series - the initial duplicating series are largely alike, though distinct between the two great kingdoms, plant and animal.

Since the life force depends upon special arrangements in the molecular universe for its manifestation, and since one characteristic of these arrangements is that matter establish a continuity of form and an ability to reproduce form, it would seem to follow that the physical laws of the molecular universe must be in some way related to a force of the non-molecular universe which has to do with establishment and maintenance of form.

One can infer the source of this second non-molecular force by looking at the smallest energized units of molecular phenomena. If we assume that the smallest unit of organized matter is the atom, we can then break it down into its three components - mass, space, and energy. Mass is clearly of matter, the molecular universe. Space, so often thought of as the absence of matter, may well be thought of as the presence of the non-molecular. It is then possible to see energy as the flow of a great force from the non-molecular universe into the molecular.

The energy which we customarily think of as being contained by matter may be better thought of as being manifested through matter. What does this energy do? On the surface, it can be thought of as an attracting and binding force, as well as a force which makes things go. But when this force is considered under the admittedly oversimplified thesis I'm advancing, it may be seen to be a shaping force, an energy configuration, of form. It serves to move units of the molecular universe into configurations which ultimately, among other things, serve as conduits for the passage of the life force. If one takes this force of configuration as a possibility, then it follows that it not only acts to give form to the molecular universe, but is the source of many of the laws affecting the molecular universe; many of our laws may thus be nothing more than unwittingly inferential statements made by intelligence about the force of configuration, the second great force of the non-molecular universe. (This thesis, by the way, makes a nice explanation for the curvature of space. If the configurational force of the non-molecular universe has no aggregated matter into which to flow, yet exists, as nothing, then the curvature of that space can be thought of as stored, meaning unmanifested configurational energy, which would reasonably be expected to produce the mathematical phenomenon of space curvature, the curvature of nothing.)

So we now have an image of two great non-molecular forces operating in the universe of matter -the configurational force which, among other things, serves to move matter into forms amenable to the flow of the other great force, that of life.

The reversal of these forces gives us, among other things also, death. If life is the condition whereby the configurational force operates to hold in place and arrangement the various energy levels of the life force, then it is reasonable to assume that if the configurational force, by any of a variety of processes, shifts its manifestation in such a way that the holding capability of the organism moves outside of acceptable limits, the life force will cease to be manifested. By analogy, all matter stores energy, but will store or release energy dependant upon a combination of internal and external conditions. If the matter in question moves or decays outside of the range of its holding capacity for one kind or level of energy, then its holding powers are lost and the energy seeks another manifestation, or vessel. This is only an analogy to the release of the life force, because non-life energies in the molecular universe are thought not to be created or destroyed, only to shift form or manifestation, while the life force must be thought of as coming and going, from and to the non-molecular universe and leaping around from organism to organism.

No moment in life is the object of more agonized spiritual questioning than death, yet in how few cases is the moment of conception examined for complementary spiritual implications. Death may perhaps be more profound because it represents the termination of the life experience, but it strikes me as absurd that it is expected that answers to the origin and thus the destiny of the life experience should be sought in its extermination alone. The accumulated image-wisdom of humans expresses a feeling for the wholeness of the birth-death continuity of process. The images of life rising from dust and returning to dust are profound. The images of another place -often out in the sky, and beyond in the immensity - are the complementary sources of understanding. But sophisticated people know that they cannot breathe life into dust, though dust can be made of life, and our instruments tell us that heaven is not an identifiable zone in the night sky, so we feel secure in ignoring the wisdom of our race's images.

Yet it is precisely through dust that life does make its entrance, or, more precisely I believe, it is through a specialized agglomeration of dust moved by the force of form, and it is precisely into the immensity of the non-molecular universe, which is everywhere and no place in the molecular universe, that the life force which is individually manifested departs. In this universe we come from dust and we go to dust; in birth we come from heaven and to heaven we go in death - the heaven-source of life, the non-molecular universe.

There are a lot of curious phenomena which appear to be aspects of the life force manifested without benefit of the configurational force ghosts and spirits, for instance. Yet it is worth noting that ghost-spirit manifestations never claim never to have lived in the body, that is, without having had a molecular manifestation. It seems imperative that the life force, in order to emerge as an individualized persona, must have been, one time at least, manifested in the flesh. On another side of the question, there is some evidence that the life force manifested in one person may remain individualized even after the death of that person's body, and that this same bundle, if you will, of life force flows into and out of a sequence of beings, a series of lives.

When one moves to consider the realm of life force as individualized spirit, one moves close to the question of whether or not the nature of the life force is perceivable by living people.

A fundamental assumption about the molecular universe holds that it is in a continuous, increasing state of disorder. This entropy, however, is not absolute; matter does spontaneously arrange itself in patterns of increasing order. Such occasions mark the appearance of Maxwell's Demon, whose effects upon the universe Professor George Gamow calls statistical fluctuations of destiny.

But it seems to me that not all entropy-reversal is random, that at least some psychic phenomena are entropy reversals taking place under the influence of the mind. The web of matter yields, on occasion, in strange ways. It has been transformed, annihilated, animated, transmuted, burned, thrown, luminesced and disassembled at various times by the psychic forces of the mind. Since psychic force, in at least some cases, is sufficient to reverse a fundamental condition of the molecular universe, it seems reasonable to conclude that the mind either is, or is connected to, a source of energy which is independent not only of the physical organism but also of the molecular levels which define its existence. What the mind does with this energy is another matter. It may be that the mind engaged in psychic work does not project energy; rather that it attunes itself to some appropriate energy level or energy sequence which affects units of the molecular universe in extra-normal ways.

If psychic phenomena may be thought of as reasonable arguments that the mind is involved with energies which, when tapped, operate without reference to fundamental conditions of the molecular universe, then we may move even closer to an understanding of the forces involved through looking at the mind in dream, because here, I think, the mind-awareness is floating freely in an uncommitted, equilibrium state, in effect between the two universes, and thus lies intermingled with the energy flows of each, and of both.

I'm not in a position in this short paper to cite phenomena which lend the dream to this particular characterization. It simply seems odd to me that we people translate the waking state into realities, and the dream state into non-reality entities, interludes in the life experience of the molecular universe which are never considered as entry into a universe from which real energies come. We live as biological beings in a universe which impinges upon our bodies, and are thus locked into assuming that since life flows into and out of our bodies, and that since life is demonstrably dependent upon the state of our bodies for effective manifestation, then dreaming is only something which our minds do, not something which we are - we believe that only our bodies are. We do not see that we exist in at least two universes; we do not see that our life comes from, and our being is a reciprocity between two universes, a reciprocity established for the maintenance of life, and in support of its destiny.

As surely as we are evolving toward a physical, biological destiny or perhaps we are flowing toward it - we are certainly moving toward a mind destiny which is the growing tip of life in this region of the molecular universe. That seems clear. But I'm not sure that human mind destiny is only to become smarter and more efficient at pushing back when the cosmos pushes. I am made very suspicious by the assumption that the dream state is treated only as a repository of little stories whose significance, if any, is tied to the waking state. The dream state experience simply doesn't impress most people as being as real as the waking state. Granted, the dream state is cluttered up with all kinds of material - stories, shadows, labyrinthine life games, ego work and ego noise - but behind all this clutter there is the state itself, which almost always goes unnoticed. There are grand dreams that take you there but which allow you to deal only in allegory, symbol and metaphor with the reality of the state which meshed so well with our waking state realities that we do not understand what they are, or often even that they are there at all.

It seems reasonable to ask whether the existence of the dream, and not its nature, character or connection with the waking state, is more significant for the understanding of life, and what we are of life. People have been so taken by the fascinating scenario played out by dreams that they have assumed the existence of a dream state but have not often looked into the state itself, other than to chart physical corollaries.

But maybe since the dream exists, and is real, and is as much a part of life if not of the physical world and its events, then maybe we ought not to pass by the chance that the dream state may be a window onto another equally real universe. Just because bright lights glitter and dark shapes loom in the interstices between the two universes, and just because we rarely go into the interlaces unless wrapped in protective illusion, does not mean that reality ends when we sleep.

Many kinds of experience argue for the existence of this reciprocity, this passing-through of a molecular and a non-molecular universe. The dream. Drug experience. The psychic phenomena. Many others. But even such experience misleads, when the person involved assumes, without noting the assumption, that the experience is only a matter of levels, and does not consider that it may be a matter of universes, within which flow vast energies of life and form. There is a difference between thinking of a higher level of the physical universe, and considering that there may be another, equally real universe whose energies are a part of your life experience. Just because forces of the molecular universe can make big rocks, push them around, and burn them up does not mean that the molecular universe is real and the non-molecular unreal.

Drug experience is something very different from the dream state it is probably another window altogether. The drug experience requires the willed use of an agent, a drug. And the will to any experience is always complicated by human follies and foibles. Drug experience is frequently in the nature of revelation, but the revelations of the drug experience are very difficult to relate to much of the true pragmatism of existence, of life as a person, now. Imposed upon the difficult-to grasp nature of the perceptions which sometimes derive from the drug experience, the act of will which led to the experience often is perverse and ego-ridden; all of which means that it is at least as hard to make sense out of a drug experience as it is out of a dream.

The dramas played out with our drugs and in our dreams may be the armor that our person, which is ego, and more, takes along as it moves closer to the window for a look at the shadowed universe which is the other side of life.

It seems reasonable that dreams, drug experiences - all the ways in which people advance toward contact with, and eventual wisdom about the non-molecular universe - should be another sort of evolutionary process. Mind evolution is usually thought of as an intergenerational IQ contest; but perhaps the purpose of life is simply to bring about unity between the two universes. In that case the race would need not only brains but also perceptivity and deep, personal understanding. And when viewed from this perspective, an awful lot of what life is doing through us as humans, is moving us forward in perceptual ways.

I'm sort of assuming that anyone is allowed to use evolution as an image in writing about things like the meaning of life. I certainly couldn't pass any exams on evolutionary theory, but since evolution of the mind is an important assumption for me, let me explain a part of what I'm talking about when I use the image.Plant life offers rich opportunities for contemplation in search of the force of life, and drug plants as a class even offer us perceptual access to the original nature of that force. I see this as a natural reading of standard evolutionary processes, which, briefly, by way of laying the foundation in the final part of this essay, I understand to go something like this. The evolutionary thesis holds that life began as small molecular manifestations which were properly neither plant nor animal. Diversification and complexity of function increased in these initial organisms as a result of environmental opportunity, pressure from resources and other organisms, and genetic change.

Selective pressures were set into process as one organism group became adept at either offense in search of food or defense in protection of life. Adept organism groups propagated similar organisms, with emphasis on the adept characteristics. Increasing diversity of organisms came about through the geometrically increasing possibilities for effective offense or defense.

As life forms became more diverse, organism groups which had developed out of the interface with original sets of antagonists and protagonists came into contact with novel life forms. Some of these encounters were very sharp. Such encounters, often correlated with environmental shifts, had dramatic consequences, leading to the extermination of whole lines of life forms and the inordinately strong stimulation of others.

This is a very simple view of evolutionary process, but sufficient to make my point which is that evolutionary theory generally does not consider the process of assimilation of one creature by another.

This omission seems to me to be significant, particularly when one considers the remarkable differences between plants and animals and looks to evolution for a rationale.

For all practical purposes, plant life has remained essentially unchanged since the beginning of the fossil record. What changes have occurred has been due largely to environmental and resource shifts. Animal life, on the other hand, has undergone vast and drastic changes in form, behavior and capability, often without respect to environmental or resource changes. Clearly there are forces at work in animal life which do not manifest in plant life, and I'm not at all sure that the difference can be successfully explained by pointing out that plants lack teeth, and can't run about chasing or being chased.

After all, the purpose of animal activity involving all this biting and hurrying about is largely the pursuit of food, which in turn involves the process of assimilation of food. And nowhere in evolutionary theory is consideration given to the process of assimilation of one organism by another, except insofar as nutrition is seen to play an important role.

However, we may recall that plants feed much, much differently than animals. Their life base is not the bodies of other organisms. They draw upon the elemental base of the earth for their nutrition, upon the carbon atoms of the air for their structure, and upon the radiant energy of the stars for their metabolic fire.

We can see, too, that of the forms of animal life which feed upon plants, few have experienced as radical an evolutionary change throughout history as have those which feed upon other animals. Aggressiveness and passivity in the arena of competitive pressures certainly play a part, but does it make sense to ignore the implications of the assimilative process in looking at the development of creatures over time?

If specialized conditions in the molecular universe are the prerequisite for the passage of the life force into that universe, then when one organism assimilates another the predator is, on one level, altering the physical nature of his being in ways which are directly related to the nature of the being which is consumed. Both are life pathways. The more complex the nutrient base of an organism, the more complex and varied the organisms which are consumed and, in turn, the more complex their nutrient base had been. The longer the food chain, the more intervening life pathways exist between the predator at the far end and the elemental base which is the beginning of life flow in the molecular universe. Since there are few if any intervening organisms in the nutrient base of

plants, it follows that if there is any relationship between the processes of assimilation and the clarity and strength of a primary flow of life energy, then plants would be receptors of a purer, far less modified flow of life energy than would be the case with animals, and especially humans.

Plant life, with its uncomplicated primary relationship to the life force, is absolutely essential and vastly beneficial to human life. One of the most enduring ways in which plants have related to man's development aside from serving as a base of nutrition, has been in their role as chemical agents for the alteration of perception. Drug plants possess compounds which clear a chemical path to that part of the human brain which is capable of elevating the mind's perceptivity to a level where it can begin to encompass non-molecular energies and focus. The path to be cleared must be chemical because that is the state in which the organism exists. The path is cluttered because the system has for all of its life been nourished with the pathways of countless beings. In this sense, perhaps the evolution of the body and that of the mind are at odds - the body taking in a rich - perhaps too rich mélange of other bodies and beings in its passage upon the earth, and the mind fighting against the weight of all these assimilated organisms which inhibit a direct, perceiving relationship with the primary forces of the non-molecular universe which form and animate the body. Those plants which give us the chemical thrusters which burn away or clear aside the clutter of our physical system are perhaps nature's compensation, life's compensation, for the physical requirements of growth and sustenance of the organism. (An equivalent, or analogous process seems to be at work with the fast. The accumulated clutter is slowly burned away while no new clutter is added, with the end result that in about forty days the path to perceiving intelligence is cleared.)

So since it seems to make sense that we beings who are at the growing tip of life's force, and are flowing toward at least a localized version of life's destiny, which is a union of the two universes, we must be involved in perceptual evolution as the non-molecular parallel of physical evolution, the purpose of which is clearly centered on cerebral development.

I think we may assume that there are perceptual as well as sensory/ physical polymorphisms in our human population. The question then becomes, which perceptual development sequences will have the strength to dominate the future growth of humankind. If there is a usefulness in the sort of thinking advanced in this commentary, it is to open people up to acts of will which enhance their humanness. The drug experience is at the center of so much of the work which people undertake when they deal with the nature of their being and their universe. Whatever else drugs may be to people and to the social body, they are also one of our windows upon the nature of what we are, and where, and maybe even why.

The mind is the channel for the manifestation of the spirit in life. The linkage between the mind and the force of spirit, or life, is that awareness is an important step on the path to unity, which is the greatest of themes in human affairs, a reflection of its primary role in the great, powerful sweep of life. So often this reflection is embodied as an image in its own right - the unity of the collective unconscious.

The image is taken from the assumption that we humans are somehow more together at an unconscious level than we are in our awareness, our consciousness. But what if the energy of life is becoming in consciousness, and yet only striving in our unconscious. The spirit which flows like a stream into being seeks like water to pool at the deepest levels. But if this pooling is not what is, but what is yet-to-be, then we all unknowingly err in our aspirations toward unity of consciousness, since we make our images in contrast to a falsely interpreted unity of the unconscious.

Not all perceptions which are entered upon are of the perceiver the dreamer, the metaphysician, the mystic, the drugged. The explorer of rivers does not question the separateness of his boat from the waters, nor does he confuse his being with the power of the flood. It is an illusion of people entering upon profound perception that it is of human province and origin, while men entering the cosmos in a ship disclaim any such presumptuousness. It is dangerous not to; failure to disclaim infallibility when tempting the highly contingent universe of matter is to invite death. Yet people often enter into the dream, the vision, the perception with the conviction that it is theirs, and therefore not contingent except as they are contingent.

I have a little shadow that goes in and out with me; and what can be the use of him is more than I can see.

One of the deep fears of dying is that of loss of awareness. Yet every thing we sense of awareness tells us that it transcends physical being. Still, we have scant evidence of any form of survival of anything we identify with our lives; what evidence we have is enough only for the most hopeful. Maybe that's because we are not paying attention in the right ways to what we already know.

Consider the myth of salvation; what it may express if we turn our perception of the nature of life around as I've tried to do in this commentary. Consider; if the collective unconscious of mankind is less together than our conscious, which isn't awfully together itself at this point, and if life's energies seem to be working toward togetherness, and since humans are the only creatures we know of who are potentially capable of unity at both levels, then maybe salvation - the remanifestation of individual consciousness, as it is seen - will finally be known through some collective awareness of life as a force which is seeking through individuals but toward transcendence of the necessity that individuals be born, and die. Perhaps we live once, to go into death as a state where the individual consciousness hasn't the strength to be self-aware any more. Perhaps salvation of the human race does not await a messiah, but the evolution of perception; perhaps on salvation it will know itself, allowing that all that will be, shall be; perhaps separate manifestation will no longer be seen as separate existence, neither will living be seen as separate from dying and death.

Whether or not an individual achieves perceptual breakthrough is only as important as the collision of one set of energy particles in a mass of fissionable material which is all at once at the critical state. The release of great energy occurs when enough atomic units are engaged in release, not together, but in concert. The achievement of critical mass in human perceptual evolution - which will release energies the like of which this region of the molecular universe has probably never seen before - should occur when enough people become aware of the other side of reality and are then in a state of being which is in accord with an integration of universes.

We probe the cosmos with radio telescopes and transmitters. Yet we are certainly being noticed by other races already; we are simply not together with them. We will only attract real attention, and an invitation to join the universal community, when we become universal ourselves. Our humanness is a stage in life's local manifestation, a stage which is at once a dramatic test and a period of preparation for universality. Life is grand. It has been striving forever, and everywhere, in a molecular universe which seems endless in all dimensions. Our human evolution to universality, significant as it must seem to us in contemplation of our destiny, is surely only a part of life's striving toward the universal integration of universes. How many integrating races on how many worlds will life itself need to reach critical mass? What a fine thought.

We worry considerably about who we are and where we are going as individuals. Upon rare occasions we even ponder where we are going as a people. But it seems to me that the question of what life is, and where it is going, should be the primary focus of our energies. Our responsibility is surely to live in the best interest of life itself, that it may evolve through us.

Maybe that is where the great energy of people lies. If life, through the human mind, can not only organize awareness but also can bring people into harmony with their nature so that their minds, instead of engaging in largely random activities, called psychic, are attuned to the collective nature of their source and their power, then perhaps at that point life will be poised to explode beyond the physical universe, and mankind will have its salvation, in a unity of life, not with life. If the evolution of perception is allowed as an attribute, not of increasingly aware individuals, but of life itself, expressing its urge toward destiny through human beings, in a process which is parallel to and complementary to physical evolution, then we open ourselves to the full knowledge that we are together, and are only together, as God, which is life.

Index To Contents

Alkaloid, 101, 102
Almazigos, 59
antidote, 47
Arab, 29
Ayurvedic, 29, 30, 31
Balkan, 3, 82
Balouchistan, 3, 11
Basket, 3, 21
Beegah, 103
bhang, 22, 155
Botanical, 3, 38, 54, 60
Brazil, 37, 55, 57, 58
British, 32, 38, 99, 100
Broadcast, 85
Broomrapes, 147
Buddha, 76
Bulgaria, 4, 80, 96
Butter, 12, 153, 154, 155, 156
Cannabis, 1, 3, 15, 22, 29, 33, 34, 35, 153, 154
Capsules, 4, 79, 92, 93, 144
Caribbean, 57
Central Bureau of Narcotics, 101
Chandu, 99, 100
Charas, 12, 13, 22, 156
Charles Fauvel, 40, 44
Chator, 6, 7, 8
Chewing, 43
Chittack, 124, 136, 138
Chuspa, 151
Climate, 80
Coca, 2, 3, 1, 2, 3, 37, 38, 39, 40, 41, 42, 43, 44, 45, 46, 47, 48, 49, 50, 51, 52, 53, 54, 55, 56, 57, 58, 59, 60, 61, 62, 63, 64, 65, 66, 67, 68, 69, 70, 71, 72, 73, 74, 75, 150, 151, 152
Coca cocaspada, 66
Coca del dia, 66
Coca leaf, 55, 56, 64, 66
Coca leaves, 3, 37, 41, 42, 43, 47, 48, 51, 55, 59, 61, 62, 72, 151
Coca seeds, 63, 67, 72
Coca tree, 2, 38, 58, 59, 72
Coffee, 45, 52, 53, 54, 57, 58, 63, 66, 90, 154
Cordillieras, 59
Cottah, 103
Crickets, 149
Cultivation, 2, 3, 4, 14, 58, 61, 68, 72, 76, 80, 82, 83, 84, 88, 100, 107, 108
Cuqui, 68
Cuzco, 57, 58
Deegah, 4, 102, 103, 107, 108, 110, 114, 119, 122, 126, 131, 132, 134, 135, 136, 138, 139, 143, 148
District Opium Officer, 101

Dragons, 3, 4
Drugs, 32, 158
Drying, 3, 9, 10, 12, 18, 60, 65, 66, 74, 75, 82, 91, 96, 116, 125, 128, 139
Earth, 3, 61
Egypt, 153
Egyptian, 3, 23
English, 22, 50
Erythroxylon, 3, 37, 38, 54, 55, 57, 58
European, 3, 37, 40, 103, 104, 106, 113, 115, 116, 117, 118, 119, 132, 133, 134, 139, 141, 146
Flower, 142
Flowering, 7, 12, 15, 17, 19, 20, 33, 76, 83, 86, 104, 105, 133, 134, 153, 154, 155, 156
Flowering, 87
Folk medicine, 30
Gangrene, 106, 139, 146, 147
Ganja, 3, 6, 12, 15, 16, 18, 22, 33
Gardens, 4, 38, 60, 107, 122
Gathering, 3, 60
Germination, 4, 115
Harvest, 3, 4, 74, 98, 144
Harvesting, 3, 4, 64, 65, 73, 93
Hash, 3, 11
hashish, 3, 9, 22, 23, 31, 154, 156
Hashish, 3, 9, 22, 23, 31, 154, 156
Hashish-zahra, 23
Hemp, 32, 33
Himalayan, 3, 12, 13, 21
Himilayas, 12, 13, 154
Inca, 37
Incision, 84, 85, 87, 93, 94, 95, 97, 98
Incision, 94, 96
Incisors, 98
India, 3, 4, 1, 5, 6, 13, 16, 17, 18, 20, 21, 29, 30, 31, 38, 88, 90, 97, 98, 100, 101, 102, 117, 128, 139, 148, 153, 155
Indians, 4, 41, 42, 46, 49, 50, 57, 64, 65, 150
Indica, 3, 25
Indigenous, 23
Insects, 4, 146
Irrigated, 15, 86, 115
Irrigation, 4, 110
Jamaica, 37
Java, 38, 70
John Scott, 100
lanced, 119, 131, 135
Latex, 90, 91, 93, 94, 95, 97
Leaf production, 70
Lebanon, 3, 9, 38
Llipta, 150, 151, 152
Mariani, 3, 59, 71, 72

Mats, 8
Maund, 103
Medical, 3, 29, 52
Medicinal, 3, 40, 76
Montana, 58, 62
Morphia, 88
Morphine, 140, 141
mould, 62, 74, 106, 147, 148
Muslim, 30
Mysore, 3, 13, 18
Nonimattee, 123, 131, 134
Opium, 2, 3, 4, 1, 2, 3, 5, 77, 78, 79, 80, 81, 82, 83, 84, 87, 88, 89, 90, 92, 93, 95, 96, 98, 99, 100, 101, 102, 140, 146, 147, 148, 149, 150, 152, 156
Opium Manual, 147, 148
Organized medicine, 34
Passewa, 96
Patna, 88, 89, 98
Peronospora arborescens, 147
Peru, 37, 38, 42, 50, 55, 57, 58, 59, 60, 62, 67, 68, 70, 73
Peruvian Venus, 44
Pests, 3, 67
Petals, 92, 93
Petechia, 147
Physician, 22, 27, 41, 47, 54, 154
Picking, 65
Pit-planting, 3, 18
Plantations, 59

Poppy, 3, 4, 2, 5, 76, 77, 78, 79, 80, 81, 82, 83, 87, 88, 89, 98, 100, 111, 128, 138, 142, 146, 152
Potency, 3, 22, 73
Predators, 3, 67
Pruning, 19
Puerto Rico, 37, 38
Pussewa, 4, 105, 106, 122, 139, 140
Quid, 40, 150, 151
Rain, 76
Resin, 25
Ridging, 15, 88
Rodents, 88
Scleriasis, 147
Season, 4, 111, 114, 116, 119
Seed, 4, 82, 98, 115, 144
Seer, 103
Soil, 4, 82, 84, 93, 95, 108
Sowing, 4, 83, 114
Stamens, 40, 56, 79
Tea, 45, 52, 53, 54
Therapeutic, 3, 72, 153
Thinning, 87
Turkey, 4, 83, 84, 85, 93, 94, 98, 116, 118, 132, 139, 142
Varieties, 4, 90, 119
Variety, 137, 141
Von Tschudi, 48, 49
Weeding, 87
Yarkand, 3, 12, 13
Yugoslavia, 4, 82, 83, 97
Zahret-el-assa, 23

Made in the USA
Columbia, SC
08 March 2018